Chicano
EATS

Chicano EATS

Recipes from My Mexican-American Kitchen

Esteban Castillo

HARPER DESIGN

An Imprint of HarperCollinsPublishers

✳ CONTENTS ✳

Introduction

Growing up in Southern California, I spent a lot of time shuttling between Mexico and the US throughout my childhood. I often heard my mom and dad repeat the same stories over and over, as if they were discos rayados, or scratched vinyls, on a constant loop. My papá would tell of his younger days as a soccer player, sneaking out of the house with nothing but a few pesos in his pocket and the huaraches on his feet to play in tournaments all over Colima, Mexico, the province where both of my parents were born. When he wasn't telling us about his childhood, he was spending his evenings after work listening to old cassette tapes that he'd buy en el swapmeet, featuring musicians like Chelo, Las Jilguerillas, and Pedrito Fernandez, reminiscing about the life he left behind when he came to the US, only to realize that the American dream he had once been enchanted by was a distant reality for him. My mom, on the other hand, always had stories on the ready about her trips to Cuyutlán, a tiny pueblito along the Pacific coast where they serve the best ceviche I've ever had, and where she and her siblings would visit every spring to help mi abuelito Rogelio mine sea salt.

It's as if they reminisced every time they needed to feel closer to home, and this habit seems to have sunk into my bones—lately I've found myself replaying their stories in my head, mixing their tales with my own daydreams of the sights and sweet smells from my trips to Mexico as a kid.

One of my favorite stories took place during a hot and sticky summer in Colima, the kind where humidity kisses every inch of your body and you're drenched in sweat the second you step out of the house. Known for its humid weather, pozole seco, and its famous palmeras (palm trees), Colima is a small state along Mexico's central Pacific coast, bordered by the states of Jalisco and Michoacán. Mi mamá said I must have been two or three, and she and I were living with mi abuelita Victoria at the time while my dad was in the States working at a warehouse building car sensors, trying to earn enough money so we could return there, too. This particular morning, everyone was helping to prepare the house for a cousin's birthday party, but I was busy watching cartoons. My mom claims that she was so busy that morning barriendo y trapeando el piso that when she looked over her shoulder, I was no longer on the couch. She wondered if I had walked over to play with the cotorras, my grandma's parrots, or if I had wandered into my aunt's room. But I had gone to neither—she found me that morning in the kitchen, of course, hiding in an olla pozolera, the pot in which my grandma would be cooking the pozole later that afternoon. If you've ever seen these ollas, you'd know that they are as wide and tall as a toddler, making them, in my case, the perfect hiding spot.

Mi mamá spotted my head peeking out of the pot, and when she turned her back, I tried climbing out to run away but fell out of the pot and cut my head open instead, leaving a scar that is still visible to this day. Now that I'm an "adult" who lives in his kitchen, I like to think that, much like the scar on my forehead, my passion for food (and hiding in the kitchen) has been etched into me since I was a little boy.

My parents immigrated to the United States in the late '80s while they were both still in their teens. They had grown up a few blocks from each other in Villa de Alvarez, Colima, and eventually met when they were both in school. My dad, the second youngest of seven, already had a few siblings who had made the trip across the border into California, and every time they spoke, these siblings would entice him with the many job opportunities that waited on the other side. Right before I was born, both of my parents decided to make the arduous trip across the border so that they could provide me with a better life. They wanted to give me everything they never had, like the possibility of a better education and healthcare. They wanted me to have the opportunity to thrive. But after I arrived, trying to establish roots in a foreign country proved very tough without a car or a decent paying job.

They decided that my mom and I would return to Colima for a bit while my dad searched for a job that would allow him to support the three of us, and so we flew to Colima to stay with mi abuelita Victoria for the next two years. Then we returned to the US again, and for my parents, this would be for good—because they were both undocumented (and

couldn't return to Mexico). I'd often find myself traveling to Mexico with an aunt or an uncle and sometimes even by myself, carrying a letter in my pocket with my parents' permission to fly alone: They wanted me to be able to enjoy what they couldn't, the privilege of traveling back to Mexico to be with family.

For my mom's side of the family, food wasn't just nourishment—it was, and still is, their livelihood. Mi abuelito Rogelio spent his life mining sea salt in Cuyutlán every spring. During the rest of the year, if mi abuelito wasn't making a giant pot of birria (a goat stew in a spiced guajillo broth) for someone's party, he'd park a clunky white taco cart outside of el jardín de la villa to sell tacos. When I had nothing better to do, I'd go sit on an empty crate by his side and scarf down his tacos de adobada with frijoles de olla and wash them down with an ice-cold orange Fanta as he sold tacos deep into the night. There was always a buzz of people walking by, greeting him with a wave and an excited "¡Órale Don Rogelio!," and crowding around his cart to wait for the prize, watching the adobada, a juicy marinated pork that was his specialty, sizzle on the flattop griddle.

After he was thrown off his horse in the cobblestoned streets of the neighboring province of Comala and injured his back, mi abuelito Rogelio had to retire, and mi abuelita Nina took over. Mi abuelita has been making cheeses for more than twenty years. It's a skill she probably picked up from one of her comadres, but we'll never know for sure because as my friend Thelma says, she's a regular "Juana of all trades." I remember I would sit in the kitchen, mostly because that's where she'd have the fan running, and I'd just watch her stand at the sink squeezing out the whey to make cheese, completely mesmerized by the process. There was something soothing about the sour smell of dairy in the air and the pit-pat sound her hands would make as she carefully molded the curds into a wheel the size of my head, wheels that would take her days to make using the milk from mi abuelito's cows. She still continues to work, opening her home to the public on weekends and transforming her backyard into a makeshift restaurant, frying up tacos de papa, sopes, and pozole seco for anyone looking for a good meal.

This back and forth between the US and Mexico continued until I was about ten years old, when I stopped visiting Mexico—I didn't get to return until I was twenty-five. My dad had changed careers as I was heading into middle school, and the next few years were a rough time for us financially. I also soon had two younger siblings growing up alongside me, so the only way I'd be returning was if I paid for the trip myself. It took, well, a while.

I decided to visit mis abuelitos for my twenty-seventh birthday because my grandpa had just experienced a stroke that left him with temporary memory loss. My grandma said that whenever he would step out of the house, he would call every man he'd pass Esteban, and it hit me right in the gut. It made me think back to those starry humid nights with the smell of sizzling adobada en la plancha in the air when I was a little kid with not a single care in the world. During this visit, I wanted to make sure I got to spend as much time with him as I could. I sat down to share a beer with mi abuelito while mis tías tried to teach my partner, Billy, a few words in Spanish. It was a warm Saturday afternoon, and my grandma was over in the corner cooking for a few guests who had shown up to have

tacos and pozole. I found myself entranced by her hands once again, as I had throughout my childhood. With no hesitation, she'd dip her fingers into the popping hot oil as she lay the tacos to fry. It was a display of bravery that made me appreciate the plates she served that much more, a sense memory that has always stayed with me.

When I moved from Santa Ana, near Los Angeles, where the Hispanic community was very alive and vibrant, to Humboldt County in Northern California to finish college, I found myself stranded in the middle of the majestic redwoods, where the Hispanic community was almost nonexistent. If I wanted a good authentic Mexican meal, I had to travel five hours south to San Francisco, and if I wanted a good home-made meal, it was twelve all the way back to Santa Ana. Needless to say, my options were slim, and homesickness (and hunger) was starting to settle in. I'd be driving home from school and I'd play songs from Lorenzo Monteclaro and Pedrito Fernandez with the windows rolled down all the way. Singing along, I would think about my parents' stories and instantly feel closer to them, but also extremely hungry. Something was missing: a really good home-cooked meal.

After settling into my new home in Humboldt, I started calling mi mamá to inquire about her recipes because I really missed her cooking and I also wanted to impress my partner, Billy, who just so happened to be a really good cook. I was desperate to make her albóndigas or her famous frijoles puercos, but she was never able to give me a full list of ingredients, let alone definite measurements. It's just not how she learned to cook. All she'd say was, "hechale un poquito de esto y del' otro," or "add a little of this and a little of that." Having made these dishes so many times before, her hands instinctively knew what to do, and how much of each ingredient to use. This was great for her, but it didn't really do much for me—I was stuck trying to put a puzzle together with way too many missing pieces. If I was going to decipher her recipes, I knew I was just going to have to dive in headfirst and get my hands, and a few dishes, very dirty.

The first recipe I ever attempted on my own was chiles rellenos. It was one of my favorite dishes as a kid because my mom always filled them with handfuls of queso fresco, and I was always amazed by how the egg whites grew taller and fluffier by the minute as she beat them with her old batidora. I called her one day, hopeful that she'd be able to share her recipe with me, but all I got was a list of ingredients with instructions foggier than San Francisco Bay. I got into the kitchen that afternoon, intimidated but hopeful, and with a little prayer to la virgencita, a miracle happened—it felt like I had made chiles rellenos before. The motions felt familiar, natural. I knew just how long to blister the chiles, how much salt to add to my batter, and my hands knew just which ingredients to reach for to create a rich and smoky salsa on which to rest the chiles. It was like I, too, had gone on autopilot while I was cooking, and before I knew it I was about to fry these beautiful little cheesy envelopes covered in fluffy egg whites. I've come to understand that recipes have been part of an oral tradition in communities like mine, and I'm part of a generation that is writing them down for future generations.

I started to realize that I loved being in the kitchen because I got to discover new ingredients, as well as rediscover old ones that I had never been particularly fond of before. (I'm looking at you, epazote!) There was something comforting and therapeutic about putting my hands to work, and learning how to make family recipes was just the type of self-care I needed at the time. I found myself using food as a portal to introduce others to Mexican culture, and as a way to feel closer to my roots in a community where I tended to be the only Latino for miles. Whenever I got the chance, I'd use birthdays and holidays as an excuse to showcase some of my concoctions and favorite recipes, and I kept surprising myself with how great dishes kept coming together with very minimal instruction. To my even greater surprise, everyone always seemed to really like my sopes or my tacos de papa, and I felt like I was that much closer to earning my badge in the kitchen.

Inspired by these early successes, trips to Colima, and the complete absence of any authentic Chicano and Mexican food anywhere in very very Northern California, not to mention no place at all to find many of the recipes I grew up with online, I took matters into my own hands. I initially created my blog, *Chicano Eats*, as a way to document recipes, share some of my favorite stories, and showcase a perspective and a heritage that were glaringly missing on the Internet. The Chicano Experience through *my* Chicano experience. I wanted to offer an alternative point of view, that of an artistic queer brown boy who grew up in California, who enjoys playing with colors and food, who can't stop eating and feeding others, and who wants to bring in as many people as possible to experience his culture through some of his favorite dishes.

From the beginning, it was important to me to showcase Chicano cuisine, Mexican cuisine reimagined through a Mexican-American point of view and pantry. It's taking ingredients and dishes we've grown up with, like chilaquiles, which are normally made with fried tortilla strips, and swapping them out for Doritos like they do at Amor y Tacos. Many, especially in California, have fallen in love with Chicano cuisine through restaurants like Cafe Cultura and their Bubulubu Frappe, uni tacos from CaCao Mexicatessen, or abalone pozole from Taco María. Being Chicano inspired me to look at food through a different lens. I thought to myself, *Does the food I make always have to be "traditional"?* And for me, the answer was *No*.

We'll start with the basics, where I'll guide you through essential recipes for dishes like arroz rojo, frijoles de la olla, los frijoles puercos de mi mamá (refried beans with chorizo, shredded carrot, and garlic), mole, a variety of BBQ sauces, and my favorite salsas. Although these recipes are very simple, they are very important, because when I was growing up, there would be days when we'd have to make meals out of many of these, like a pot of beans and rice with warm tortillas and a fresh salsa de molcajete. Many of these will also accompany a lot of dishes throughout the book.

Botanas, or appetizers, are the stars of chapter 2. In this chapter you'll find recipes for dishes you can share con tus tíos y tías, los primos, la vecina, and all of your best friends. As someone who loves to host for the holidays, I like to have an arsenal of small bites up my sleeve to keep everyone's pancitas (bellies) happy while the main course is finishing up.

From there, we'll get into tacos and tortas, including recipes for my juicy and crispy carnitas, or mi abuelito's tacos de adobada, chile-marinated pork tacos that I have enjoyed since I was a kid. Next up is platillos fuertes, dishes you can make during the week for dinner, or make during the weekend to enjoy con la familia. In this chapter you'll find comforting dishes like mis chochoyotes con chicken, a version of chicken and dumplings made with soft corn masa dumplings called cho-

choyotes. I also have not just one, but three different recipes for pozole!

Later chapters focus on my favorite part of a meal: dessert. I have a really big sweet tooth, so I wanted to make sure all of the treats I enjoyed as a kid were present one way or another! In this chapter you'll find several recipes for cakes and gelatinas (gelatin desserts that mi mamá always made for our birthdays), inspired by childhood favorites like my Duvalín jello, an ode to the brand of neapolitan frosting candy that always made its way into piñatas. Growing up in Southern California, where the weather was always nice and warm year-round, we used paletas (ice pops) and ice cream to cool off! I'm including several recipes for granitas, or adult raspados, like my refreshing melon granita made with fresh watermelon and cantaloupe juice, or my horchata granita that you can serve at your next dinner party with a shot of dark rum.

We'll finish up with a variety of drinks, including recipes for many different aguas frescas that you can enjoy year-round, like my cherry lime chia agua, which combines sweet dark cherries with fresh tart lime juice that can easily be turned into a cocktail. You'll also find recipes for basic aguas like agua de jamaica, strawberry agua fresca, horchata, and some fun twists like the coconut horchata, strawberry jamaica, and tejuino, a masa-based drink with roots in pre-Columbian Mexico!

The recipes in this book are meant to be a reflection of my bicultural upbringing, weaving in and out of borders, just like I did. They're a reflection of a community, que es ni de aqui, ni de alla, who's neither from here nor there, whose "authentic" is true to the neighborhoods and sorrundings they grew up in but comes together in shared experiences. I hope this book inspires you to learn how to make traditional Mexican dishes that you might not be familiar with and cook with friends or family. I also hope it sparks old memories as well as helps make new ones, but, most important, I hope you enjoy cooking your way through my Chicano eats.

The Essentials

Jardín de la Villa (2016)

If you come over to visit me on any given night, you'll immediately be greeted by my three dogs, Nomi, Jepsen, and Rigby, who will try to win your heart over with their big wet sloppy kisses and beautiful big brown eyes. After they're done catching your attention, you'll probably notice the smell of warm frijolitos simmering on the stove.

Open up my fridge, and you'll notice leftover arroz con frijoles, plenty of salsa (de la que pica, of course!), queso Oaxaca for those nights when I've had one too many micheladas and I'm craving a quesadilla, queso Cotija for those early morning chilaquiles, a never-ending supply of avocados and cilantro, and if you're lucky, you might stumble upon my secret Flamin' Hot Cheetos stash in the pantry, for when I'm having a hot Cheeto emergency (which seems to happen every other day). These things never change, because these items are the backbone of a lot of the dishes I like to make.

Throughout this chapter I'll be walking you through everything I keep stocked in both my fridge and my pantry regularly—various spices, herbs, chiles, and cheeses—as well as important recipes for essential building blocks, like frijoles de la olla, arroz rojo, salsa de molcajete, mole coloradito, and a few BBQ sauces that will be used throughout the book. Now that I've stirred up your appetite, let's talk about cheese!

CREMA
MEXICANA

QUESO
OAXACA

AÑEJO

QUESO
FRESCO

CREMA
ÁGRIA

QUESO
COTIJA

PANELA

Quesos

CHEESES

Queso is crucial to my dishes because I often use it to season, especially if the cheese is salty. Different types of cheeses have varying uses, so let's take a look at the different cheeses I like to keep on hand.

QUESO FRESCO: Queso fresco is a creamy fresh cheese with the texture of feta when in a wheel, but ricotta when crumbled. It is typically used for chiles rellenos, breakfast tacos, and huevos rancheros.

QUESO COTIJA: Cotija, named after the pueblito in the state of Michoacán, is a hard and salty cheese, similar to Parmesan. It is great for crumbling on sopes, huaraches, and refried beans. Feta is a good substitute for Cotija.

QUESO OAXACA: This creamy, semihard cheese from the state of Oaxaca is a cross between mozzarella and string cheese and is often found wrapped in a ball. It is great for melting, making it perfect for quesadillas. Mozzarella is a good substitute for queso Oaxaca.

PANELA: Panela is semihard cheese that is very salty, creamy, and dense, similar to halloumi. Panela is great for throwing on the grill, because the outside will crisp up but not melt. Halloumi is a good substitute for panela.

AÑEJO: Añejo is a salty, dry, hardened cheese that has been aged and rolled in dried ground chile powder. Queso añejo is also crumbly, making it perfect for topping tostadas, tacos dorados, refried beans, and enchiladas. Romano and Parmesan are substitutes for queso añejo.

CREMA MEXICANA: A rich table cream similar to crème fraiche used to drizzle over tacos dorados, flautas, chiles rellenos, or elotes preparados.

CREMA ÁGRIA: Mexico's sour cream is much tangier and thicker in consistency than Crema Mexicana. It is also used as a topping for enchiladas, tacos, and soups.

Chiles

Chiles are present in just about everything I make. Chiles aren't always used to add hot spice to a dish; instead, seeded chiles are often used in base dishes for their flavoring, and the spice is then incorporated into sauces. Fresh chiles like jalapeños and serranos add an earthy layer to different salsas, and roasted poblanos, toasted chiles de árbol, and chipotle chiles infuse a sweet smoky punch to sauces. Here are the chiles we'll be using throughout the book.

GUAJILLO: The guajillo chile is the dried form of the mirasol chile. It is one of the more commonly used chiles in Mexican cuisine, because it is very fruity, but not very spicy. Guajillos are typically used in adobos, pozole rojo, moles, and sauces and can be located in the spice aisle or the Hispanic section.

JALAPEÑO: Jalapeños are green and red in color, but traditionally found as the green variety. They have a very crisp bite and earthy taste and are very versatile. Roasted jalapeños are perfect for salsa de molcajete, and they can also be pickled and served on tacos, tortas, sopes, and refried beans or used fresh. Jalapeños are widely available across the US in the produce section. A smoked dried jalapeño is a chipotle (see below).

POBLANO AND ANCHO: Poblano chiles are very mild in taste, and when dried they are known as chiles anchos/ancho chiles. They are typically used to make sauces and salsas, and are often roasted to be used in chiles rellenos. Fresh poblanos can be easily found in grocery stores around the American Southwest; in other regions, you'll have to locate your nearest Mexican grocery store. Dried ancho chiles are much more common than their fresh counterpart, located in either the spice aisle or the Hispanic section.

SERRANO: Serrano chiles are green in color and look similar to a jalapeño, with a very crisp bite and earthy taste to them. They are considerably hotter than a jalapeño, are used in salsas and pico de gallo, and are widely available fresh in the produce section.

ÁRBOL: Chile de árbol is a small red chile that packs a heat punch and is widely used in Mexican cuisine. Toasted, it becomes very aromatic and adds an extra layer of flavor in a roasted salsa. It is often sold in bulk, and can be found in the spice aisle or the Hispanic section.

CHIPOTLE: Chipotles are jalapeños that have been smoked and dried and typically canned in a smoky adobo sauce. They are also sold dried (not canned in adobo), but are much harder to come by. Chipotles not only add spice, but they also add smokiness. They are typically used in adobos, sauces, and salsas, and in dishes like the Cemita sandwich. Chipotles in adobo are widely available in the canned vegetables aisle, or the Hispanic section of your local grocery store.

HABANERO

CHIPOTLE

ÁRBOL

POBLANO

JALAPEÑO

GUAJILLO

SERRANO

Tortillas

When I'm shopping for tortillas, I tend to stay away from the more well-known brands. They're mass produced and often have a lot of additives that make them taste sour. Search the Hispanic foods aisle of your supermarket for tortillas made by local or smaller vendors—they're going to be a lot more fresh and more flavorful. The tortilla is an important vessel, so you want to make sure you are able to taste the corn and not the additives. If you're looking for flavor, reach for yellow corn tortillas; white corn tends to be more subtle. If you'd like to make your own and don't have access to a store that carries fresh masa, you can find masa harina online and in the Hispanic foods aisle. Making your own tortillas gives you the freedom to infuse your tortillas with different spices and herbs, and allows for tasty experiments!

There are two pieces of equipment associated with making tortillas at home, a tortilla press and a comal. Tortilla presses can usually be easily found online or at your local Hispanic supermarket. I prefer to use a metal tortilla press over wood, as it keeps longer and takes up less space. The comal is a flat round skillet (which you can find on Amazon or at your local Hispanic supermarket) used to cook tortillas or sopes, but a large skillet will also work in a pinch.

Herbs and Spices

Herbs are what really round out a dish. Whether they are dried or fresh, they all help in bringing out different flavors and adding complexity to any dish. Here's some of what I like to keep on hand.

CILANTRO: Also known as fresh coriander, cilantro is a very fresh and crisp herb. It is sometimes used as an aromatic, as in Frijoles de la Olla (page 33), but for the most part, it is used fresh to add a crisp and citrusy taste to salsas, tacos, and just about any other dish.

MEXICAN OREGANO: This is an herb that I like to use as an aromatic in broths, sauces, and adobos, especially in al pastor, pozole, and menudo. It packs a bigger flavor punch than Mediterranean oregano and is almost always used dried. Before you use it, be sure to rub it between your palms to "wake" it up.

CINNAMON: When I use cinnamon, I like to reach for sticks of Mexican canela (Ceylon cinnamon) and grind them myself. There is nothing more satisfying than grinding your own spices and reaping the added benefit of having them fill your kitchen with their gorgeous aromas.

MINT: Fresh mint brightens up sweet and savory dishes, but I really enjoy using it in aguas frescas, where it heightens the flavors of the ripe fruits.

THYME: Thyme is a delicate herb that I like to use for its aromatic properties. It adds a beautiful layer to a lot of the adobos I make, and it is very prominent in adobos for tacos de adobada and tacos Tuxpeños. I prefer to use fresh thyme, but dried thyme works in a pinch.

CUMIN: Ground cumin is a spice that I don't often use, but when I do, I use it sparingly. Use too much and its very strong punch will overpower your dish.

CLOVES: I like to use little dried clove buds to season adobos and moles. Adding a few cloves to a pork adobo helps bring out the natural sweetness in the meat.

TAJIN: This is a chili lime seasoning that is often used to sprinkle over fresh fruit and esquites, to rim glasses for cocktails, and to season proteins like fish or chicken. It's my go-to seasoning when something needs a boost of a familiar flavor.

PILONCILLO

MEXICAN OREGANO

CILANTRO

MEXICAN CINNAMON

BAY LEAF

DRIED HIBISCUS

SEA SALT

MEXICAN CHOCOLATE

SCALLION

TOMATILLO

COMAL

MOLINILLO

TORTILLA WARMER

JARRITOS

MOLCAJETE

OLLA DE BARRO

LIME JUICER

Tools

COMAL: This is a flat, typically round skillet used to cook tortillas and things like sopes, huaraches, and gorditas.

TORTILLA PRESS: Sometimes wooden, aluminum, or cast iron, used to flatten masa to make tortillas or sopes.

LIME JUICER: A handheld citrus juicer.

MOLCAJETE: A mortar and pestle made from volcanic rock used to make salsas or grind spices.

OLLA DE BARRO: A clay pot typically used to make things like frijoles de la olla, Mexican hot chocolate, atole, and even guisados.

MOLINILLO: A wooden whisk used to mix and froth Mexican hot chocolate.

TORTILLA WARMER: A basket used to keep tortillas warm.

JARRITOS: A clay mug or cup.

Resources

MEX GROCER
- Spices
- Dried chiles
- Fresh specialty produce
- Mexican candy
- Mexican cooking tools

mexgrocer.com

MASIENDA
- Masa harina
- Heirloom corn

masienda.com

SIETE FOODS
- Alternative flour tortillas (like cassava flour or almond flour)
- Vegan-friendly dips and sauces
- Hot sauces
- Grain-free tortilla chips

sietefoods.com

LA TORTILLA FACTORY
(my favorite tortillas)
- Non-GMO tortillas
- Organic wraps
- Low-carb tortillas
- Protein tortillas

latortillafactory.com

RANCHO GORDO
- Heirloom beans
- Hominy
- Dried chiles
- Herbs and spices
- Sauces

ranchogordo.com

Salsa de Molcajete

A good salsa de molcajete is like a little black dress: It's versatile! Ground in a molcajete, a traditional Mexican mortar and pestle made from volcanic rock, this chunky and smoky salsa made from roasted tomatoes, toasted chiles de árbol, and fresh onion and cilantro is perfect on fried eggs, chilaquiles, a bowl of frijolitos, tacos, or a quesadilla. If you don't have a mortar and pestle, this can easily be made in a food processor.

INSTRUCTIONS

Preheat the broiler. Line a baking sheet with foil. Arrange the tomatoes skin side up on the baking sheet and broil on the top rack until the skins blacken and blister, about 10 to 12 minutes. Set aside to cool.

Meanwhile, in a dry skillet, toast the chiles over medium heat for 1 minute, flip them, then toast for 1 more minute.

Add the garlic, toasted chiles, and salt to a molcajete or large mortar. Use the piedra or pestle to grind everything together until a paste is formed. Add the blistered tomatoes, one at a time, and grind them into the paste. Add the lime juice, half of the diced onion and half of the chopped cilantro and then use a spoon to mix everything together. Add salt to taste. Top the salsa with the remaining diced onion and chopped cilantro, and serve with tortilla chips.

FOOD PROCESSOR SALSA

Follow the recipe through toasting the chiles, then add all of the ingredients to the processor and pulse until everything has been fully incorporated, but is still slightly chunky.

1 pound (455 g) Roma (plum) tomatoes (about 3 to 4), halved lengthwise

3 chiles de árbol, stemmed (use 4 for more heat)

3 garlic cloves, peeled

½ teaspoon Diamond Crystal kosher salt, plus more to taste

1 tablespoon (14 ml) fresh lime juice (from ½ lime)

¼ white onion, diced

¼ cup chopped fresh cilantro

Tortilla chips, for serving

4 jalapeños, cut crosswise into slices ¼ inch (6 mm) thick

½ large white onion, sliced

1 large carrot, peeled and cut crosswise into coins ¼ inch (6 mm) thick

3 garlic cloves, peeled and lightly smashed

1 teaspoon dried Mexican oregano

1 large bay leaf

1¼ cups (295 ml) distilled white vinegar

1½ tablespoons Diamond Crystal kosher salt

Jalapeños en Escabeche

PICKLED JALAPEÑOS WITH CARROTS AND ONION

Jalapeños en escabeche are those pickled jalapeños you're typically served when you order tacos at your favorite taqueria. They're really easy to make and customize with your favorite veggies: This is the classic escabeche mix, but feel free to use any mix of vegetables with the jalapeños, making sure you've got 4 cups (480 g) vegetables total (cauliflower florets and fresh green beans would be a great addition). If you'd like to go the nacho ring route, then just omit the carrot and onion and instead use 4 cups (480 g) sliced jalapeños.

INSTRUCTIONS

In a 1-quart (1 liter) mason jar, place the jalapeños, onion, carrot, garlic, oregano, and bay leaf.

In a medium saucepan, combine 1 cup (240 ml) water, the vinegar, and salt and bring to a boil over high heat, stirring to make sure the salt has dissolved. Once it's boiling, remove the pan from the heat and carefully pour over the vegetables in the jar.

Lightly press down the vegetables to make sure everything is submerged and let cool to room temperature before placing the lid on the jar. You can store the jalapeños in the refrigerator for up to 2 weeks.

Salsa Trio

My favorite salsas are the ones you can pour into a bowl and snack on with tortilla chips. These three salsas are great on tacos, burritos, and chips, and are especially perfect for those nights when all you want to do is binge on Netflix after work with an ice-cold Michelada (page 195)!

Salsa de Aguacate
AVOCADO SALSA

Makes about **3 cups** *(710 mℓ)*

INSTRUCTIONS

Scoop the avocado flesh into a blender or food processor. Add the garlic, green onion, tomatillo, cilantro, serrano, lime juice, 1½ cups (355 ml) water, and salt and blend until smooth. Adjust the salt to taste. Transfer to a serving bowl and serve with tortilla chips.

2 avocados, halved and pitted

3 garlic cloves, peeled

1 Mexican green onion (or 2 small regular green onions), roughly chopped

1 tomatillo, husked and rinsed and cut in half

¼ cup (10 g) cilantro leaves

1 serrano chile (seeded if you don't want it as spicy)

¼ cup (60 ml) fresh lime juice (from about 2 limes)

2 teaspoons Diamond Crystal kosher salt, plus more to taste

Tortilla chips, for serving

Roasted Salsa de Chipotle

Makes **1½ cups** *(355 mℓ)*

INSTRUCTIONS

Preheat the broiler. Line a baking sheet with foil. Arrange the tomatoes, skin side up, and the green onions on the baking sheet. Broil until everything has an even char, 10 to 12 minutes, flipping the onions at the 6-minute mark. Let the tomatoes and onions cool down for a bit.

In a blender or food processor, combine the tomatoes, onions, garlic, chipotles, cilantro, lime juice, and salt and blend until smooth. Adjust the salt to taste. Transfer to a serving bowl and serve with tortilla chips.

(continued)

1 pound (455 g) Roma (plum) tomatoes (about 3 to 4), halved lengthwise

2 Mexican green onions (or 3 small regular green onions)

3 garlic cloves, peeled

2 chipotle peppers in adobo sauce

¼ cup (10 g) fresh cilantro leaves

2 tablespoons fresh lime juice (from 1 lime)

1 teaspoon Diamond Crystal kosher salt, plus more to taste

Tortilla chips, for serving

1 pound (455 g) tomatillos, husked, rinsed, and halved

2 Mexican green onions (or 3 small regular green onions)

2 garlic cloves, peeled

1 serrano chile, seeded

¼ cup (10 g) fresh cilantro leaves

1½ teaspoons fresh lime juice (from 1 lime)

1 teaspoon Diamond Crystal kosher salt, plus more to taste

Tortilla chips, for serving

Salsa Verde

Makes 1½ cups (355 ml)

INSTRUCTIONS

Preheat the broiler. Line a baking sheet with foil. Place the tomatillos skin side up on the baking sheet. Broil until they all have an even char, 10 to 12 minutes. Let the tomatillos cool.

In a blender or food processor, combine the tomatillos, green onions, garlic cloves, serrano, cilantro, lime juice, and salt and blend until smooth. Adjust the salt to taste. Transfer to a serving bowl and serve with tortilla chips.

Frijoles de la Olla

STOVETOP BEANS

Makes 6 cups (1420 mℓ)

When I was growing up, it seemed like mi mamá had a never-ending supply of frijoles stashed in her pantry, because there was always a pot of frijolitos with sweet onions and fragrant cloves of garlic simmering on the stove. Dining out was never something we did, so whenever we dared to ask for a treat while we were out and about, we could always count on hearing, Espérate, hay frijoles en la casa (Wait, there are beans at home). Now, a bowl of frijoles de la olla is a sweet reminder of home to me, and of how my mom always made sure we had something in our bellies. Traditionally, frijoles de la olla are made on the stovetop, but I've included directions for the pressure cooker, which is my preferred method. The beans cook in a third of the time, and I find that the pressure cooker infuses the aromatics into the beans much more, producing a more flavorful broth and beans.

INSTRUCTIONS

Start by quick-soaking the beans. Rinse and drain the beans, making sure to get rid of any broken beans and rocks that might be in the batch. In a 6-quart (6 liter) Dutch oven or stockpot, combine the beans and 4 cups (1 liter) water and bring to a boil over medium-high heat. Immediately remove from the heat, cover, and let them rest for 1 hour.

Drain the beans (discard the soaking liquid) and return the beans to the pot. Add the onion, garlic, cilantro, thyme, bay leaf, and lard. Pour in 9 cups (2.13 liters) water. Bring the beans to a boil over medium heat, then reduce the heat to medium-low and simmer, uncovered, for 30 minutes.

Season the beans with the salt, then reduce the heat to low, cover, and continue to cook until the beans are creamy and tender, about 2 hours 30 minutes. Remove and discard the onion, garlic, cilantro, thyme stems, and bay leaf before serving. Adjust the salt to taste.

Serve the beans in a bowl with some of the broth, queso fresco, chopped yellow onion, cilantro, and warm tortillas.

(continued)

1 pound (455 g) dried pinto beans

¼ yellow onion

5 garlic cloves, peeled

⅓ cup (15 g) fresh cilantro (about one small bunch with stems included)

2 sprigs fresh thyme

1 bay leaf

1½ teaspoons lard

1½ teaspoons Diamond Crystal kosher salt, plus more to taste

Queso fresco, chopped yellow onion, cilantro, and corn tortillas, for serving

MAKING BEANS IN A PRESSURE COOKER

Rinse and drain the beans, making sure to get rid of any broken beans and rocks that might be in your batch. Skip the quick-soaking step and transfer the beans to a pressure cooker. Add the flavoring ingredients as above, using only 8 cups (1.9 liters) water. Close the lid and switch the valve to seal. Set the pressure to high and set the cooking time to 45 minutes. When the timer goes off, let the steam release naturally for 10 minutes, then quick-release the remaining pressure. Use a slotted spoon to remove the onion, garlic, cilantro, thyme stems, and bay leaf before serving. Add salt to taste.

Frijoles Charros

COWBOY BEANS

Frijoles charros are Mexico's version of cowboy beans, and depending on who's making them, you may receive a bowl with ham, bacon, or sliced hot dogs in them. My version is sweet and smoky, with notes of smoked paprika and spicy chipotles, and tons of crispy bacon and longaniza, a cured pork sausage similar to chorizo. Traditionally, the meats are cooked with the beans, but I prefer to cook most of it separately and top the beans with the meats so they stay crispy.

INSTRUCTIONS

Start by quick-soaking the beans. Rinse and drain the beans, making sure to get rid of any broken beans and rocks that might be in the batch. In a 6-quart (6 liter) Dutch oven or stockpot, combine the beans and 4 cups (1 liter) water and bring to a boil over high heat. Immediately remove from the heat, cover, and let them rest for 1 hour.

Meanwhile, in a large Dutch oven or soup pot, melt the lard over medium-low heat. Add 3 whole slices of the thick-cut bacon and the yellow onion and cook until the onion starts to turn translucent, about 5 minutes. Stir in the garlic, then mix in the diced tomatoes and chipotle and cook for 5 minutes. Sprinkle in the chipotle pepper adobo, smoked paprika, coriander, cumin, and ½ tablespoon kosher salt. Let simmer for 5 more minutes, then remove from the heat.

Drain the beans (discard the soaking liquid) and stir them into the pot with the tomato mixture. Pour in 8 cups (1.9 liters) water and bring to a boil over high heat. Cover with a lid, then reduce to a simmer and cook until creamy and tender, 2 hours 30 minutes to 3 hours. Add salt to taste.

Once the beans are done cooking, start frying up the meats. Dice the rest of the thick-cut bacon. In a large skillet, cook the bacon over medium-low heat until it reaches your desired crispness, 10 to 12 minutes. Drain off the fat and set the bacon aside.

In the same skillet you cook the bacon, cook the longaniza over medium heat, using a spatula to break it into smaller pieces as it cooks, until browned, 10 to 12 minutes. Drain and set aside.

To serve, ladle the frijoles charros into a bowl with some of the broth, then top with cooked bacon, longaniza crumbles, onion, cilantro, jalapeños, and crumbled cheese. Serve with tortillas.

1 pound (455 g) dried pinto beans

1 teaspoon lard

1 pound (455 g) thick-cut bacon

1 yellow onion, diced

5 garlic cloves, finely minced

1 (28 ounce/794 g) can petite diced tomatoes

1 chipotle pepper in adobo sauce, finely chopped

1 tablespoon chipotle pepper adobo

½ teaspoon smoked paprika

½ teaspoon ground coriander

½ teaspoon ground cumin

Diamond Crystal kosher salt

12 ounces (340 g) longaniza sausage, casing removed

Diced onion, cilantro, sliced serrano, radish, avocado, and corn tortillas, for serving

Serves 5 or 6

Frijoles Refritos

REFRIED BEANS

Frijoles refritos, or refried beans, are one of my favorite things to have in the fridge. Aside from using them to accompany dinner, you can also heat some up throughout the week and spread them on a tortilla with a smoky salsa de molcajete for taquitos de frijoles, or spread some over a toasted bolillo and add a sprinkle of queso cotija for a quick torta.

INSTRUCTIONS

In a large skillet, melt the lard over medium heat. Add the diced serrano and diced onion and fry for 5 minutes, stirring occasionally.

Add the minced garlic to the pan and cook for 1 more minute, then add the beans 2 cups (340 g) at a time, and mash them completely with a potato masher before adding the next batch. Repeat this process until you have incorporated all the beans. Add some of the reserved cooking liquid to loosen them up to your desired consistency, making sure you add only a few tablespoons of liquid at a time so they don't end up being too runny. Use an immersion blender to blend the beans for smooth texture.

Cook the beans, stirring constantly, until fully warmed through, 5 to 6 more minutes. Remove from the heat and season with salt.

Serves 6 or 8

1½ tablespoons lard

½ small yellow onion, diced

1 serrano chile, stemmed and finely diced

2 garlic cloves, finely minced

6 cups (1 kg) Frijoles de la Olla (page 33) plus 2 cups (473 ml) bean cooking liquid

Diamond Crystal kosher salt

Mi Mamá's Frijoles Puercos

MY MOM'S PORK REFRIED BEANS

Serves 6 or 8

Los frijoles puercos de mi mamá are, in one word, amazing. Whenever she makes them for a get-together, I try to be the first to sneak in with Tupperware to make sure I get leftovers, because they always disappear quickly. Frijoles puercos are essentially refried beans cooked with longaniza (or chorizo), sweet carrots, onion, and diced tomato, and it is a recipe that I really cherish because it is one of the dishes my mom is known for, and it was one of the very first recipes she ever shared with me. Frijoles puercos are perfect with Birria and Arroz Rojo (page 43), or spread on a toasted bolillo topped with salty queso Cotija for a simple torta.

INSTRUCTIONS

In a large skillet, heat 1 tablespoon of the lard over medium heat until it sizzles. Add the chiles de árbol and cook for 2 minutes on each side to infuse the lard. Remove the chiles and set aside (leave the fat in the pan).

Add the onion, carrot, and diced tomato to the same skillet and cook until the onion starts to turn translucent, about 5 minutes. Add the longaniza and cook, using a spatula to break the sausage into smaller pieces, until the sausage has browned, about 10 minutes.

Stir in the remaining ½ tablespoon of lard, then season with ½ teaspoon kosher salt. Lower the heat to medium-low then add the cooked pinto beans 1 cup (170 g) at a time, and mash them completely with a potato masher before adding the next batch. Repeat this process until you have incorporated all the beans. Add some of the reserved cooking liquid to loosen them up to your desired consistency, making sure you add only a few tablespoons of liquid at a time so they don't end up too runny.

Add salt to taste and sprinkle crumbled Cotija cheese over the beans, then garnish with the fried chiles de árbol.

1½ tablespoons lard

2 chiles de árbol

1 small yellow onion, diced

1 carrot, peeled and finely shredded

1 (14.5 ounce/411 g) can petite diced tomatoes

12 ounces (340 g) longaniza sausage, casing removed

Diamond Crystal kosher salt

6 cups (855 g) Frijoles de la Olla (page 33) plus 2 cups (473 ml) cooking liquid

Cotija cheese, crumbled, for serving

Arroz Rojo

RED RICE

Serves
4 or 5

Arroz Mexicano, or arroz rojo, is a big staple in Mexican cuisine. It can seem like a daunting task to make rice, but if you follow a few basic steps, you will end up with fluffy, flavorful rice every time. The beautiful thing about arroz rojo is that you can easily make it your own with a few simple additions.

INSTRUCTIONS

In a large skillet, heat the oil over medium heat. Add the garlic and rice and cook, stirring frequently, until the rice is fragrant and lightly toasted, 3 to 4 minutes.

In a small bowl or measuring cup, stir together the chicken stock, tomato paste, onion powder, coriander, cumin, and pepper. Pour the mixture into the skillet and bring to a full boil. Stir in the mixed vegetables, then reduce the heat to low, cover with a tight-fitting lid, and cook for 15 minutes. Remove from the heat and let the rice slt, covered, to steam for an additional 15 minutes. Uncover, let the steam release for 5 minutes, then fluff with a fork, and season with salt to taste. Serve alongside your favorite dishes!

1 tablespoon neutral oil, such as canola or vegetable

3 garlic cloves, finely sliced

1 cup (185 g) long-grain white rice

1⅔ cups (395 ml) chicken stock, warmed

4 tablespoons tomato paste

1½ teaspoons onion powder

½ teaspoon ground coriander

¼ teaspoon ground cumin

¼ teaspoon freshly ground black pepper

½ cup (65 g) frozen mixed vegetables (or substitute with fresh or frozen yellow corn)

Diamond Crystal kosher salt

Serves
4 or 5

Arroz Blanco

WHITE RICE

2 tablespoons (30 g)
unsalted butter

3 garlic cloves, finely sliced

1 cup (180 g) basmati
or long-grain white rice

1¾ cups (415 ml) chicken
stock

½ cup (70 g) yellow corn
kernels, fresh, canned,
or frozen

Diamond Crystal
kosher salt

Arroz blanco is the buttery and garlicky cousin of Arroz Rojo (page 43). It reminds me of the many bus trips I took as a little boy with mi abuelita Victoria to Tecomán, where we often had mojarras fritas (a delicious fried white fish) with arroz blanco at the ramadas, or food stalls, by the ocean. Arroz blanco is just as easy to make as arroz rojo, and I find that using basmati rice makes this dish even more fragrant and flavorful.

INSTRUCTIONS

In a large skillet, melt the butter over medium heat. Add the garlic and rice and cook, stirring occasionally, until the rice is nicely toasted and the garlic is fragrant, 3 to 4 minutes.

Stir in the chicken stock and bring to a full boil. Stir in the corn, then reduce the heat to low, cover with a tight-fitting lid, and cook for 15 minutes. Remove from the heat and let the rice sit, covered, to steam for an additional 15 minutes. Uncover, let the steam release for 5 minutes, then fluff with a fork, then season with salt to taste. Serve alongside your favorite dishes!

Mole

Mole, pronounced "mo-lay," from the Nahuatl word *mōlli* for "sauce," is a very rich and complex sauce that contains many ingredients. My version has a nice balance of sweet and savory with a fiery orange hue, similar to mole coloradito, one of the seven different mole sauces from Oaxaca.

Makes 7 1/2 cups (1.75 liters)

INSTRUCTIONS

In a large bowl cover the peppers and raisins with 5 cups of boiling water. Set this aside while the peppers soften.

In a large non-stick skillet, melt down the lard over medium heat. Add the plantain, onion, garlic, almonds, sesame seeds, cloves, and peppercorns. Fry up the ingredients, stirring occasionally to make sure nothing burns or sticks, until everything is golden brown and toasted, 10 to 15 minutes. While this toasts, blend the tomatoes in a blender until smooth, 20 to 30 seconds, then add them to a large Dutch oven or stockpot.

Once the ingredients have toasted add them to the blender with the chicken stock and the softened peppers and raisins (making sure to reserve the soaking liquid) and blend on high for a full minute with the center portion of the lid removed and a towel covering it to make sure nothing explodes if the mixture is too hot.

Once blended, strain the mixture with a fine mesh sieve right into the Dutch oven or stock pot, stirring the mixture in the strainer with a whisk to help push it through. Once strained, put the pulp in the strainer back into the blender with 1 cup (236 ml) of the pepper soaking liquid and blend on high for one more minute, straining one more time into the stockpot or Dutch oven. This step is to help anything that didn't blend properly the first time break down a little more.

Add the oregano, cinnamon, panko bread crumbs, brown sugar, and salt to the Dutch oven or stockpot and bring to a gentle simmer over low heat. Cook uncovered for 1 hour, stirring about every 10 min to make sure the mole doesn't clump or burn.

After an hour, the mole should have thickened quite a bit and gotten slightly darker. Remove from the heat and add the chocolate. Taste for salt and adjust, then serve over your favorite protein.

To store, cool completely then place in an airtight container. Store in the refrigerator for up to 5 days. If storing in the freezer, let the mole cool completely then transfer to a 1-gallon (4.55-liter) zip-top freezer bag and let freeze on a flat surface. When you're ready to use the mole, defrost it in the refrigerator then heat up on the stove and use however you choose. The mole will keep for up to three months in the freezer if stored properly.

4 ancho chiles (2 ounces/56 g), stemmed and seeded

8 large guajillo chiles (about 5½ inches/14 cm long) (2 ounces/27 g), stemmed and seeded

¼ cup raisins

2 tablespoons pork lard, or neutral oil

1 medium yellow (ripe) plantain, sliced

1 yellow onion, peeled and roughly chopped

6 garlic cloves, peeled

¼ cup whole almonds

1/4 cup (35 g) sesame seeds

3 whole cloves

½ teaspoon whole black peppercorns

1 (14-ounce/397g) can whole peeled plum tomatoes

4 cups (946 ml) chicken stock

1 teaspoon dried Mexican oregano

½ teaspoon ground Mexican (Ceylon) cinnamon

3 tablespoons Panko breadcrumbs

¼ cup (50 g) light brown sugar

1 ounce (28 g) Mexican chocolate (such as Ibarra or Abuelita), roughly chopped

2 teaspoons Diamond Crystal Kosher salt, plus more to taste

BBQ Sauces

The perfect weather in Southern California means we get to enjoy carne asadas, or barbecues, year-round, and one of the ingredients that I find myself reaching for a lot is BBQ sauce. Whether I'm grilling codornices (quail) para mi mamá, or grilling chicken wings for a get-together, it's nice to be able to make my own BBQ sauces from scratch and infuse some of my culture and favorite flavors into them.

Makes about **2 1/2 cups** *(590 ml)*

Hibiscus BBQ Sauce

INSTRUCTIONS

In a medium saucepan, bring 3½ cups (830 ml) water to a boil over high heat. Remove from the heat and add the hibiscus and anchos. Set aside for at least 20 minutes to let the chiles soften.

With a slotted spoon, remove and discard the hibiscus, then add the chiles and the soaking liquid to a blender and blend on high speed for 30 seconds. Once the chile mixture is smooth and completely blended, pour the mixture through a fine-mesh sieve back into the saucepan it was steeping in, pressing on any solids left behind to make sure you get out as much flavor as possible.

Whisk the tomato paste, brown sugar, Worcestershire sauce, salt, smoked paprika, garlic powder, and onion powder into the pan and bring the mixture to a simmer over medium-low heat. Cook, stirring occasionally, until thickened enough to coat the back of a spoon, about 30 minutes. Adjust the salt to taste.

Let the mixture come to room temperature, then transfer to a sealed container. You can use this right away or store in the fridge sealed tightly, where it will keep for up to 2 weeks—the flavors develop a little more if made a day ahead.

(continued)

1 cup (35 g) dried hibiscus flowers

2 ancho chiles (1 ounce), seeded

1 (6 ounce/170 g) can tomato paste

⅔ cup (145 g) packed dark brown sugar

2 tablespoons Worcestershire sauce

2 teaspoons Diamond Crystal kosher salt, plus more to taste

1½ teaspoons smoked paprika

1 teaspoon garlic powder

1 teaspoon onion powder

Mezcal BBQ Sauce

Makes about 2 1/2 *cups* (590 ml)

3 ancho chiles
(1½ ounces), seeded

1 (6 ounce/170 g) can
tomato paste

⅔ cup (145 g) packed
dark brown sugar

⅓ cup (75 ml) mezcal

2 tablespoons
Worcestershire sauce

1 tablespoon apple cider
vinegar

2 teaspoons Diamond
Crystal kosher salt

1 teaspoon garlic powder

1 teaspoon onion powder

Pinch of cayenne pepper

INSTRUCTIONS

In a medium saucepan, bring 2⅔ cups (630 ml) water to a boil over high heat. Remove from the heat and add the anchos. Set aside for at least 20 minutes to let the chiles soften.

Transfer the chiles and the soaking liquid to a blender and blend on high speed for 30 seconds. Once the chile mixture is smooth and completely blended, pour the mixture through a fine-mesh sieve back into the saucepan it was soaking in, pressing on any solids left behind to make sure you get out as much flavor as possible.

Add the tomato paste, brown sugar, mezcal, Worcestershire sauce, vinegar, salt, garlic powder, onion powder, and cayenne to the pan and bring to a simmer over medium-low heat. Cook, stirring occasionally, until thickened enough to coat the back of a spoon, about 30 minutes. Adjust the salt to taste.

Let the mixture come to room temperature, then transfer to a sealed container. You can use this right away or store in the fridge sealed tightly, where it will keep for up to 2 weeks—the flavors develop a little more if made a day ahead.

Tamarind BBQ Sauce

INSTRUCTIONS

In a medium saucepan, combine 3½ cups (830 ml) water, tamarind pulp or paste, and anchos and bring to a boil over high heat. Reduce the heat to medium and let simmer for 3 minutes to ensure the tamarind softens and is able to dissolve, then remove from the heat. Set the saucepan aside for at least 20 minutes to let the chiles soften.

Using a slotted spoon, transfer the chiles to a blender. Pour the tamarind (or tamarind pulp) and the soaking liquid through a fine-mesh sieve into the blender and blend on high speed for 30 seconds. Once the tamarind-chile mixture is smooth and completely blended, pour the mixture through a fine-mesh sieve back into the saucepan it was soaking in, pressing on any solids left behind to make sure you get out as much flavor as possible.

Add the tomato paste, brown sugar, Worcestershire sauce, salt, smoked paprika, garlic powder, and onion powder to the pan and bring to a simmer over medium-low heat. Cook, stirring occasionally, until thickened enough to coat the back of a spoon, about 30 minutes. Adjust the salt to taste.

Let the mixture come to room temperature, then transfer to a sealed container. You can use this right away or store tightly sealed in the fridge where it will keep for up to two weeks. The flavors develop a little more if made a day ahead.

Makes
4 cups
(946 ml)

6 tamarind pods (shells and veins removed) or use 3½ ounces (100 g) seedless tamarind pulp

3 ancho chiles (1½ ounces), seeded

1 (6 ounce/170 g) can tomato paste

¾ cup (165 g) packed dark brown sugar

2 tablespoons Worcestershire sauce

2 teaspoons Diamond Crystal kosher salt, plus more to taste

1½ teaspoons smoked paprika

1 teaspoon garlic powder

1 teaspoon onion powder

Botanas

✳ (SNACKS AND APPETIZERS) ✳

Cancún (2015)

When I was a kid, summer was my favorite time of the year. Summer didn't just mean no school for the next eight weeks, it meant flights to Colima to visit mis abuelitos. And this meant trips to Los Amiales, the crystal-clear river in Colima, to bathe and eat mojarras fritas, delicious fried white fish; it meant eating paletas de vainilla (vanilla ice pops) en el jardín, and getting to feel the volcanic sand in between my toes in Cuyutlán. Colima is a small state in Mexico along the Pacific. It is the place where my parents grew up, the place I'd visit every February for the Fiestas Charrotaurinas (and the warm churros at the fair), the place I spent my summers growing up, and it is the place that has continually inspired me to get creative in the kitchen.

Spending time with mis abuelitos year after year taught me a lot about hospitality. Their doors were always open to their community (literally!). Friends and neighbors would often walk by and wander in to greet Papi Heyo, mi abuelito, or drop by to share a little gossip with Mami Nina, mi abuelita. Mis abuelitos would always greet their company, whether they were friends or family, with "Ya comiste?" or "Have you eaten yet?" and Mami Nina would typically whip up something quick and delicious, like picaditas or taquitos de frijoles, from whatever she had leftover in her fridge.

Hosting friends and family has become one of my favorite things to do because of them. It allows me to nourish others the same way mis abuelitos do, even if it is with a simple taquito de frijoles.

This chapter is filled with botanas, or appetizers, you can share among friends. Many of them use ingredients you might already have in your fridge and pantry, which is perfect for those days when someone drops by unexpectedly.

Mac and Queso Fundido

I have a soft spot in my heart for boxed mac and cheese because it's the only kind I ever got to enjoy as a kid. There were a few times where I'd sneak into the kitchen and try to make it myself, only to fail miserably (and I mean *miserably*). The noodles wouldn't be cooked properly because I didn't know how to boil water, the cheese sauce would often be too runny and clumpy, resulting in a crunchy and soupy concoction. So you might be wondering, what is my mac and cheese like now that I know my way around the kitchen? Well, I'd say it's delicious, it's complex, but it's incredibly easy to make.

This recipe combines two of my favorite comfort foods—mac and cheese and queso fundido—to make a dish with so many layers of flavor: The creamy cheese sauce is infused with garlic, onion, and paprika, then layered with spicy chorizo and savory mushrooms.

INSTRUCTIONS

Bring a large pot of well-salted water to a boil over high heat for the pasta.

Meanwhile, in a large skillet, heat the vegetable oil over medium heat. Add the cremini and cook until crispy and golden brown all over, about 5 minutes on each side. Season with a pinch of salt and pepper. Transfer the mushrooms to a plate.

Line a plate with paper towels. Add the chorizo to the same skillet and cook, crumbling the meat with a spatula, until the fat has rendered and the chorizo is crispy, 10 to 12 minutes. Remove and set aside on the paper towels to drain.

Drop the pasta into the boiling water and cook according to the package directions. Drain and set the pasta aside.

Meanwhile, in a large saucepan, melt the butter over medium heat. Add the garlic, stir to combine, and cook for 2 minutes. Whisk in the flour then slowly whisk in the chicken stock. Once the chicken stock is incorporated, whisk in the milk and heavy cream and continue whisking until smooth. Whisk in the onion powder and smoked

(continued)

Ingredients

- 1 tablespoon vegetable oil
- 5 ounces (140 g) cremini mushrooms, sliced
- Diamond Crystal kosher salt
- Freshly ground black pepper
- 4 ounces (115 g) fresh chorizo, casings removed
- 8 ounces (225 g) cavatappi (corkscrew) pasta
- 2 tablespoons (30 g) unsalted butter
- 4 garlic cloves, minced
- 3 tablespoons all-purpose flour
- 1 cup (240 ml) chicken stock
- ¾ cup (175 ml) whole milk
- ¼ cup (60 ml) heavy (whipping) cream
- 1 teaspoon onion powder
- ½ teaspoon smoked paprika
- 1½ cups (165 g) shredded mozzarella cheese
- 1 cup (112 g) shredded Colby Jack
- ½ cup (50 g) shredded Parmesan cheese
- 1 green onion, sliced, for serving

paprika, then return to a simmer, and cook until it begins to thicken, about 3 minutes. Remove from the heat and stir in the mozzarella, Colby Jack, and Parmesan until they are completely melted. Adjust the salt to taste (if your chicken stock and Parmesan aren't salty enough, your cheese sauce will need a pinch or two of salt here).

Add the pasta back into the large pot, then add the cheese sauce to the pasta and stir to evenly coat the pasta in the sauce. Transfer to a serving dish and top with the mushrooms and chorizo. Garnish with green onions and serve immediately.

Alitas de Gusano

TAMARIND CHICKEN WINGS

Serves 4 or 5

I was in fifth grade when my mom finally deemed me old enough to make the five-block walk home from school by myself. Every day after school I'd catch up with friends who lived along the way and we'd walk together, often stopping by las troquitas (vending trucks) lined up outside of school for Hot Cheetos, Chupa Chups lollipops (to collect Spice Girls stickers, of course), and my favorite, the Lucas Gusano candy. It is a spicy, tamarind-flavored liquid candy that comes in an accordion-shaped bottle that mimics the way caterpillars crawl, which is how it gets its name (*gusano* means "worm").

When I got older, I stumbled across the candy at the supermarket and thought to myself, *How can I re-create this and use it in a dish?* Then it hit me: chicken wings! They are the perfect vehicle for sauces, especially spicy ones. I've re-created this childhood classic with a blend of tamarind paste and ancho chiles to make a sauce that'll bring on the nostalgia with every bite. Note: I use party wings, which are already trimmed and broken down. If you can only find whole wings, simply locate the two joins on the wings and use a knife to cut at each joint for drumettes and wings, then discard the tips.

INSTRUCTIONS

Preheat the oven to 400°F (200°C).

Prepare the wings: In a small bowl, mix together the cornstarch, salt, and pepper. Place the wings in a large bowl, add the vegetable oil, and toss to evenly coat the wings. Sprinkle the cornstarch mixture over the wings and toss again to evenly coat.

Line an 18 × 13-inch (46 × 33 cm) baking sheet with foil and coat it with cooking spray. Distribute the chicken wings evenly on the baking sheet. Transfer to the oven and bake until the wings are crispy and golden, 50 to 55 minutes, flipping them over at the 30-minute mark.

Meanwhile, make the sauce: In a large heatproof bowl, cover the anchos with boiling water and let sit for 15 to 16 minutes to fully rehydrate. Drain the chiles, then stem and seed them and set aside.

(continued)

FOR THE WINGS

2 tablespoons cornstarch

2 teaspoons Diamond Crystal kosher salt

½ teaspoon freshly ground black pepper

2½ pounds (1.1 kg) chicken wings

2 tablespoons vegetable oil

FOR THE SAUCE

2 medium ancho chiles (1 ounce)

Boiling water

6 ounces (170 g) seedless tamarind pulp, broken down into 1-ounce (28 g) chunks

1 cup (200 g) sugar

1 teaspoon New Mexico chile powder

1 teaspoon Diamond Crystal kosher salt

FOR THE GARNISH

Sesame seeds

Green onion, sliced

In a small saucepan, combine 2¼ cups (530 ml) water and the tamarind chunks. Bring to a simmer over medium heat and let simmer, stirring occasionally, until the tamarind has completely broken up, 6 to 8 minutes. Remove from the heat and let cool for a few minutes.

Strain the tamarind mixture and push the solids through a fine-mesh sieve into a blender. Add the sugar, chile powder, salt, and rehydrated anchos. Blend until smooth, then strain back through a sieve into the small saucepan used for the tamarind. Simmer the sauce over medium-low heat, stirring occasionally, until it is thick enough to coat the back of a spoon, about 5 minutes. Remove from the heat.

Once the wings are done baking, use tongs to transfer them to a large bowl. Pour in the sauce and use the tongs to toss the wings. Serve on a platter and garnish with the sesame seeds and sliced green onion.

Tequila BBQ Chicken Skewers

Makes
12 Skewers
6 inches (15 cm)

I live in Southern California, where it's virtually summer year-round, and that means I get to enjoy the grill a little longer. Aside from making carne asada or grilling codornices (quails) for my mom, I love making a good chicken skewer, because it's a good app to tide everyone over while the main event finishes cooking! Juicy chicken thighs marinate in a tangy sauce for about an hour before caramelizing on the grill.

INSTRUCTIONS

In a large bowl, mix together the green onions, cilantro, garlic, salt, pepper flakes, tequila, lime juice, and ¾ cup (175 ml) of the BBQ sauce. Add the chicken thigh chunks and give them a good toss, making sure each piece is fully coated in the marinade. Cover the bowl with plastic wrap and let marinate in the refrigerator for at least 1 hour or up to overnight.

Preheat the grill to medium-high. Thread the skewers through the chicken chunks, then place them on the grill and cook until the meat is fully cooked through, 10 to 12 minutes, flipping them over once every minute. After 5 minutes, start brushing the skewers after each turn with the remaining ¾ cup (175 ml) BBQ sauce.

Garnish with chopped cilantro and serve with lime wedges on the side.

2 green onions, finely chopped

3 tablespoons chopped fresh cilantro, plus more for garnish

2 garlic cloves, minced

1½ teaspoons Diamond Crystal kosher salt

1 teaspoon crushed red pepper flakes

¼ cup (60 ml) tequila

2 tablespoons fresh lime juice (from 1 lime)

1½ cups (355 ml) Hibiscus BBQ Sauce (page 49)

2½ pounds (1.1 kg) boneless, skinless chicken thighs, cut into 2-inch (5 cm) chunks

12 (6-inch/15 cm) bamboo skewers

Lime wedges

Carnitas Poutine

Serves 6

There are times when friends or family decide to randomly stop by to visit, and it's usually when I'm really busy and haven't made anything special for dinner. It's during these times where I take a second to think: *What would mi abuelita do? She'd go into her fridge and whip up something out of nothing!* Luckily, there are a few things I like to keep stocked in my fridge at all times, like queso Oaxaca, carnitas, and mole, which is how my take on poutine—a Canadian dish typically comprising fries, gravy, and cheese curds—came to be. This dish is inspired by the mole tots from one of my favorite restaurants in Southern California, Amor y Tacos, and if you haven't already made the Mole Coloradito (page 47), I hope these fries smothered in mole topped with carnitas and queso Oaxaca inspire you to make it for this appetizer alone, which can easily turn into the perfect dinner for one after a few Micheladas (page 195).

INSTRUCTIONS

Cook the waffle fries in the oven according to the instructions on the package.

Heat up the carnitas and mole while the fries bake and keep warm until ready to assemble.

Assemble the poutine by piling up some fries on a platter, topping them with the carnitas, and then the mole. Finish with a small pile of cheese and a sprinkle of green onions.

2 pounds (910 g) frozen seasoned waffle-cut fries

1 cup (42 g) shredded carnitas (from Tacos de Carnitas, page 91)

1½ cups (355 ml) Mole (page 47)

1½ cups (165 g) shredded queso Oaxaca

Green onions, sliced, for garnish

FOR THE CHICKEN

2 tablespoons vegetable oil

2½ pounds (1.1 kg) boneless, skinless chicken thighs

1 teaspoon Diamond Crystal kosher salt

¼ teaspoon cracked black pepper

2 garlic cloves, finely minced

2½ cups (590 ml) Mezcal BBQ Sauce (page 50)

FOR THE JICAMA SLAW

¼ cup (60 ml) apple cider vinegar

Juice of 1 lime

1 teaspoon Diamond Crystal kosher salt

1 teaspoon sugar

1 teaspoon dried Mexican oregano

2½ cups (260 g) julienned jicama

½ cup (20 g) chopped fresh cilantro

½ cup (35 g) chopped red cabbage

FOR ASSEMBLY

24 mini French rolls

Mayonnaise

Mezcal BBQ Sliders with a Jicama Slaw

Makes 24 sliders

Managing your time when you're prepping for a get-together can be difficult, especially if you're cooking everything yourself—you don't want to end up stuck in the kitchen all night long! These chicken sliders paired with a fresh and crisp jicama slaw are easy enough to throw together. The recipe is really simple, and even easier if you have a slow cooker!

INSTRUCTIONS

Make the chicken: In a large Dutch oven, heat the vegetable oil over medium-low heat. Add the chicken thighs and brown them for 4 minutes on each side. Add the salt, black pepper, and garlic and cook for 1 minute. Pour in the BBQ sauce and bring to a simmer. Once the sauce starts to simmer, cover the pot and cook until the meat is fully cooked through, 40 to 45 minutes. (Alternatively, add all of the ingredients to a slow cooker, give them a stir, and cook on high for 2 hours.)

Meanwhile, make the jicama slaw: In a small bowl, combine the vinegar, lime juice, salt, sugar, and oregano and let it sit for 10 minutes. In a larger bowl, toss together the jicama, cilantro, and red cabbage. Pour in the vinegar mixture and toss to coat.

Once the chicken thighs have cooked, use a slotted spoon to remove them from the Dutch oven and shred the thigh meat in a bowl using two forks. Once all of the chicken has been shredded, return it to the Dutch oven and give it a stir to coat it evenly in the sauce.

To assemble: Slice the rolls in half and brush some mayo on each half. Toast for a few minutes in a pan, then add a spoonful of the chicken and a spoonful of the slaw to the bottom halves of each. Place the top half of the bun on and arrange on a serving platter. If you wish, stick a toothpick through the top buns to ensure the sandwiches stay together.

Flautas de Rajas con Queso

CHEESE AND POBLANO PEPPER FLAUTAS

Watching my mom cook was always a treat, literally. If I sat around to watch long enough, she'd eventually give me taquito or a spoonful of whatever it was she was making. If she was making sopes, she'd take some of the masa and use her palms to flatten and toss the masa back and forth to form a rough tortilla and cook it on the comal and fill it with queso fresco. These flautas are inspired by those simple cheese taquitos. They're filled with a mixture of queso panela and sautéed poblanos and onion, and they're the perfect finger food to share with friends.

INSTRUCTIONS

Start by heating up two tablespoons of the vegetable oil in a large skillet over medium-low heat. Once it starts to sizzle, add the sliced poblanos, chopped mushrooms, and onion, and cook, stirring occasionally, until the onion starts to become translucent, about 6 to 8 minutes. Stir in the garlic and spices and cook for an additional 2 minutes, taste the filling for salt, then adjust and remove from the heat.

Heat the tortillas in the microwave for 30 to 45 seconds. You want them to be warm so they are easier to roll. A cold tortilla will rip.

Heat ½ inch (1.25 cm) of vegetable oil in a large skillet over medium-low heat. Once it starts to sizzle, working in batches of 5 to 6, take a tortilla and add about 1 tablespoon of the sautéed poblano and onions, then add two strips of the panela cheese. Roll tightly, then place in the skillet seam side down and fry for 2 to 3 minutes on each side until golden brown. Repeat with the remainder of the tortillas.

Arrange the flautas on a platter, then top with lettuce, onion, radish, and serrano. Crumble queso fresco over the flautas and finish with a drizzling of crema Mexicana and avocado salsa.

Makes 12

FOR THE FILLING

2 tablespoons vegetable oil, plus more for frying

2 poblano peppers, stemmed, seeded, and sliced lengthwise ¼ inch (6 mm) wide

5 ounces (140 g) cremini mushrooms, chopped

½ yellow onion, thinly sliced into half moons

3 garlic cloves, thinly sliced

¼ teaspoon Diamond Crystal kosher salt

¼ teaspoon ground black pepper

¼ teaspoon ground coriander

¼ teaspoon ground cumin

8 ounces panela, cut into 4-inch (10 cm) strips, ½ inch (1.2 cm) in thickness

TO ASSEMBLE

12 tortillas

Shredded lettuce

½ yellow onion, diced

Sliced radish

Sliced serrano

Queso fresco

Crema Mexicana

Salsa de Aguacate (page 31)

Tacos y Tortas

※ (TACOS AND SANDWICHES) ※

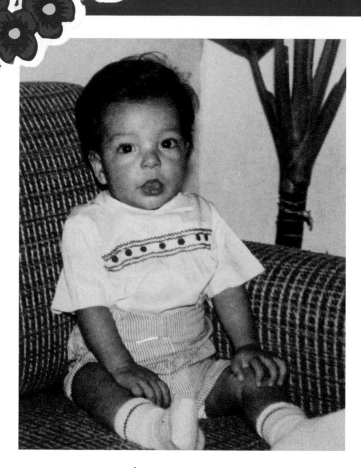

Villa de Àlvarez, Colima (1990)

When I think about tacos and tortas (sandwiches), I think about happiness. I think about the many times I spent alongside mi abuelito at his stand as he worked his charm and made tacos for a hungry crowd right outside el jardín de la villa. I think about the many trips I took to Colima when I'd sneak off to Tavo's, my mom's favorite torta joint, right before leaving for the airport to pick up a torta de lomo (a sandwich with pork braised in a guajillo salsa) to bring back to my mom so she'd be able to have a little piece of the life she wasn't able to come back to. I'm reminded of the trips to the tortillería where mi abuelita Victoria would send me to pick up fresh tortillas, and the many times I'd run to Chinta's, the little convenience store at the end of the street that my dad would frequent as a kid, with spare change to purchase an ice-cold Coke she'd serve to me in a little plastic bag with a straw. I also think about the many Sundays I'd spend with my parents in California at the ranch as a family, and the late-night trips we'd take to the taquería right after.

Tacos and tortas have always been an integral part of my life. For as long as I can remember I've had corn tortillas with every meal, making taquitos out of just about everything, and at times having to double up on them when there wasn't much to eat. En serio—my dad even likes to eat his *chicken tenders* con tortillas! Living across from a panadería and a carnicería that made their own tortillas, teleras, and bolillos meant we got to enjoy them fresh and often. If I was ever running late to school, mi mamá could throw together a quick sandwich for us using refried beans and queso fresco. Tortas were convenient, they kept well during our trips to Disneyland, or trips to my tias' dairy farm in Merced, but most important, they were inexpensive.

In this chapter, we'll be making tacos and tortas. You'll get to experience my family's famous taco recipes, including mi abuelita's tacos de papa and mi abuelito's famous tacos de adobada—a crispy guajillo-marinated pork taco that people always swarmed his stand for. We'll also be playing with different proteins, including vegetarian options, for making explosively delicious tortas. Many of these next few recipes are designed so you can use the fillings in tacos and tortas interchangeably, with many options to make both carnivores and vegetarians very happy!

Mi Abuelita's Tacos de Papa

MY GRANDMA'S POTATO TACOS

Makes
12 tacos

One of the things I missed the most about visiting Mexico was mi abuelita Mami Nina's cooking. She used to sell raspados (a shaved-ice treat made with fresh fruit syrups) and sopes on the weekends to help make ends meet. It took more than ten years to get back to Mexico, and during that first visit back, I noticed things hadn't changed: She still opens up her house on the weekends to anyone who's hungry, serving pozole, sopitos, and the crunchiest tacos de papa I've ever had, served with a big pile of lettuce and queso Cotija.

INSTRUCTIONS

Make the filling: In a large pot or Dutch oven, combine the potatoes, garlic, and water to cover by about 1 inch (2.5 cm). Bring to a boil over high heat, then reduce the heat to medium-low and simmer until tender, about 15 minutes.

Transfer the potatoes and garlic to a bowl, add the salt and pepper, and mash. Adjust the salt to taste.

Make the sauce: Wipe out the large pot or Dutch oven you used for the potatoes and add the tomatoes, onion, tomatillo, and garlic. Add water to cover by 1 inch (2.5 cm) and bring to a simmer over medium-low heat. Simmer until the tomatoes soften, 10 to 15 minutes.

Drain the vegetables, then transfer to a blender and add the chicken stock, salt, and black pepper. Blend (be sure to open the steam vent/center cap and cover with a towel to avoid explosive hot liquid) until smooth. Adjust the salt to taste.

Return the mixture to the pot, place the lid on, and simmer over medium-low heat for 15 minutes to cook the salsa through. Remove from the heat and set aside while you fry the tacos.

(continued)

FOR THE TACO FILLING

1½ pounds (680 g) Yukon Gold potatoes, peeled and cubed

5 garlic cloves, peeled

1 teaspoon Diamond Crystal kosher salt, plus more to taste

½ teaspoon freshly ground black pepper

FOR THE SAUCE

4 large whole Roma (plum) tomatoes

¼ small yellow onion

1 tomatillo, husked and rinsed

2 garlic cloves, peeled

1½ cups (355 ml) chicken stock (or sub in your favorite veggie broth to make this vegan)

¾ teaspoon Diamond Crystal kosher salt, plus more to taste

¼ teaspoon freshly ground black pepper

FOR ASSEMBLY

12 corn tortillas

Vegetable oil for fryimg

Shredded cabbage or lettuce

Sliced tomato

Diced white onion

Sliced radishes

Cotija cheese (or your favorite vegan substitute)

Hot sauce

To assemble: Working in batches of 3 to 4, pop the tortillas in the microwave for about 45 seconds, or heat them up on a comal over medium heat for about 1 minute on each side. (Cold tortillas will rip.)

In a large skillet, heat 1 inch (2.5 cm) of vegetable oil over medium-low heat. Add 2 to 3 tablespoons of the mashed potatoes to a tortilla, fold the tortilla in half, and fry until crispy and golden brown on both sides, 2 to 3 minutes per side.

Fill each taco with a little shredded cabbage and a tomato slice, then ladle some of the tomato sauce over it. Finish by garnishing with some onion, radishes, Cotija, and your favorite hot sauce.

Mi Abuelito's Tacos de Adobada

MY GRANDPA'S ADOBO PORK TACOS

The tart smell of vinegar mixed with aromatic chiles, garlic, and thyme is a distinct aroma I will always associate with mi abuelito Rogelio, or Papi Heyo as I grew up calling him, and the small taco cart he'd move around in Colima for many years. It evokes memories of a young Estebitan juggling an ice-cold Fanta in one hand and a plate of tacos de adobada in another, sitting quietly by his grandfather's side on a crate, as he watched his Papi Heyo do what he did best: nourish people's souls through food. Adobada consists of thin slices of pork—marinated in an aromatic and acidic adobo made with a mix of chiles, apple cider vinegar, fresh thyme, and garlic, among other spices—grilled on a sizzling flattop griddle and served on a tortilla that's been lightly fried and topped with fresh frijolitos de la olla.

INSTRUCTIONS

Make the adobada: In a medium saucepan, combine the guajillos and ancho, and enough water to completely submerge the chiles. Bring to a boil over high heat, then reduce the heat to low and simmer until the chiles have softened, about 15 minutes.

Use a slotted spoon to scoop out the chiles and transfer them to a blender. Add the vinegar, garlic, thyme, salt, oregano, paprika, black pepper, and vegetable oil. Blend the marinade until smooth, 20 to 30 seconds.

Cut the pork shoulder into slices ½ inch (1.25 cm) thick, then use a mallet or the bottom of a heavy skillet to pound them into a ¼-inch (6 mm) thickness.

Place the slices of pork in a 1-gallon (4.55 liter) freezer bag, add the bay leaf, then pour in the marinade and mix together to make sure all of the pork is evenly covered in the marinade. Place in the fridge and let the pork marinate for at least 4 hours or up to 8 hours.

(continued)

Serves 4 or 5

FOR THE ADOBADA

6 large guajillo chiles (about 5½ inches/14 cm long) (1½ ounces), stemmed and seeded

1 ancho chile (½ ounce), stemmed and seeded

1 tablespoon apple cider vinegar

5 garlic cloves, peeled

1 teaspoon fresh thyme leaves

4 teaspoons Diamond Crystal kosher salt

1 teaspoon dried Mexican oregano

¼ teaspoon paprika

¼ teaspoon freshly ground black pepper

1 tablespoon vegetable oil

3 pounds (1.3 kg) pork shoulder

1 bay leaf

FOR ASSEMBLY

3 tablespoons vegetable oil

Mini corn tortillas (street taco size), warmed or lightly griddled

**Frijoles de la Olla
(page 33)**

Chopped fresh cilantro

Diced white onion

Sliced radishes

Salsa

Lime wedges

Sea salt

To assemble: On a flattop griddle (or in a large skillet), heat half the oil over medium heat. Place the marinated pork on the griddle and cook until cooked through and crispy on both sides, 5 to 6 minutes per side. Remove from the heat and let the pork rest for about 5 minutes, then cut into strips ¼ inch (6 mm) wide. While the pork rests, add the remaining oil to the griddle or skillet and lightly fry the tortillas for 1½ minutes on each side. Replenish the oil as needed.

To serve, place a spoonful of the pork on a tortilla. Place a spoonful of frijoles de la olla on top of the meat, then sprinkle cilantro, onion, and radishes over the top. Serve with salsa, lime wedges, and sea salt.

Tacos al Pastor

SHEPHERD-STYLE PORK TACOS

Al pastor was brought to Mexico by Lebanese immigrants in the twentieth century, and similar to shawarma, this marinated protein is grilled on a rotating spit and pieces of meat are shaved off as needed. Al pastor has become one my favorite types of tacos to have whenever I'm visiting a new city in Mexico because everyone adds their own flair to the adobo; being able to take ideas or dishes and make them your own with what is accessible to you is one of my favorite things about food. My adobo has a mixture of guajillo, pineapple juice, fresh thyme, Mexican oregano, and plenty of achiote paste to give it a bright red hue. If you happen to have extra telera rolls in your pantry, don't be afraid to use any leftover al pastor for tortas!

INSTRUCTIONS

Make the filling: In a medium saucepan, combine the guajillos, and enough water to completely submerge the chiles. Bring to a boil over high heat, then reduce the heat to low and simmer until the chiles have softened, about 15 minutes.

Use a slotted spoon to scoop out the chiles and transfer them to a blender. Add the pineapple juice, lime juice, vegetable oil, vinegar, onion, garlic, achiote paste, thyme, oregano, salt, and brown sugar. Blend the marinade until smooth, 20 to 30 seconds.

Cut the pork shoulder into slices ½ inch (1.25 cm) thick, then use a mallet or the bottom of a heavy skillet to pound them into a ¼-inch (6 mm) thickness.

Place the slices of pork in a 1-gallon (4.55 liter) freezer bag, then pour in the marinade and mix together to make sure all of the pork is evenly covered in the marinade. Place the bag in the fridge and let the pork marinate for at least 4 hours or up to 8 hours.

(continued)

FOR THE FILLING

4 large guajillo chiles (about 5½ inches/14 cm long) (1 ounce), stemmed and seeded

1 cup (240 ml) pineapple juice

Juice of 1½ limes

1 tablespoon vegetable oil

½ tablespoon apple cider vinegar

¼ small white onion

5 garlic cloves, peeled

1.75 ounces achiote paste (half of a 3.5-ounce/100 g package)

1¼ teaspoons fresh thyme leaves

1 teaspoon dried Mexican oregano

2½ teaspoons Diamond Crystal kosher salt

1 teaspoon packed light brown sugar

2½ pounds (1.1 kg) pork shoulder

FOR ASSEMBLY

1½ tablespoons vegetable oil (optional)

Corn tortillas, warmed

Diced fresh or grilled pineapple

Diced white onion

Minced fresh cilantro

Lime wedges

To assemble: If you have a grill, preheat the grill to medium. Grill the pork until crispy and cooked through, 5 to 6 minutes per side. To cook on the stovetop, heat the oil in a large skillet over medium heat. Add the pork and cook until crispy and cooked through, about 5 to 6 minutes per side. Remove from the heat and let the pork rest for about 3 minutes, then dice, or cut into strips ¼ inch (6 mm) wide.

Serve the pork on warm tortillas and garnish with pineapple, onion, and cilantro. Serve with lime wedges.

Chorizo-Spiced Delicata Squash Tortas

Makes 4 or 6 tortas

My dad has been working in construction for most of his life, and for as long as I've known him, he has woken up at 4 a.m. every day to make the long commute to different jobs around Los Angeles. Mi mamá has woken up just as early to make sure he has lunch to take with him. Sometimes lunch would be a really simple ham sandwich on white bread with slices of tomato and a slice of American cheese, sometimes a warm bolillo with leftover beans. Other times, when there wasn't any meat or leftover proteins, she'd pack him a very basic torta with slices of tomato, crema, and queso fresco. It was so simple, yet satisfying, and it is one of the tortas that I have gone back to time and time again. Her simple torta has evolved in my hands, and now includes roasted delicata squash tossed in my very own chorizo spice blend. If you don't feel like making tortas, this recipe doubles as a taco recipe! Simply sauté the squash, toss it in the chorizo spice mix, and serve it on a tortilla with your favorite taco fixings.

INSTRUCTIONS

Preheat the oven to 375°F (190°C). Line a large baking sheet with foil.

Toss the squash with the oil on the prepared baking sheet and arrange so all the squash pieces are in a single layer, not overlapping. Roast the squash for 20 minutes. Carefully flip each piece and roast until the squash is cooked through and golden brown, 15 to 20 minutes longer.

In a large bowl, lightly toss the roasted squash with the chorizo spice mixture and allow to cool slightly before assembling the torta.

To assemble: Spread mayonnaise on each half of a telera, then place a few slices of tomato and a small pile of squash on the bottom half of the telera. Sprinkle crumbled Cotija over the squash then finish with a drizzle of crema, then place the top half of the roll on top.

(continued)

FOR THE FILLING

2 (1 pound/453 g) delicata squashes, halved lengthwise, seeds scooped out and sliced into ½-inch (1.25 cm) half-rings

2 tablespoons olive oil

2 tablespoons Chorizo Spice Mix (recipe follows)

FOR ASSEMBLY

Mayonnaise (or your favorite vegan substitute)

4 to 6 telera rolls, halved and toasted

Sliced tomato

Crumbled Cotija cheese (or your favorite vegan substitute)

Crema Mexicana

4 large guajillo chiles (about 5½ inches/14 cm long) (1 ounce)

1 ancho chile (½ ounce), stemmed and seeded

1 tablespoon Diamond Crystal kosher salt

1½ teaspoons granulated garlic

1½ teaspoons granulated onion

½ teaspoon smoked paprika

½ teaspoon ground cumin

⅛ teaspoon ground allspice

⅛ teaspoon ground cinnamon

⅛ teaspoon ground cloves

Chorizo Spice Mix

INSTRUCTIONS

Preheat the oven to 275°F (135°C), then place the chiles on a baking sheet, and bake for 10 minutes.

Add the peppers to a spice grinder or a high-powered blender and grind them down until you get an even, granulated consistency. Then place in a jar with a tight-fitting lid.

Add the salt, garlic, onion, oregano, smoked paprika, and ground spices to the jar with the ground peppers, place the lid on, and shake to combine. This spice mix can be stored in a cool, dry place for up to 3 months.

Makes about 1/3 CUP (40 g)

Roasted Sambal Shrimp Tacos

Serves
4

Sambal oelek is a really spicy chile sauce from Southeast Asia. It's usually used as a condiment, and it pairs really well with seafood. For these tacos, I marinated shrimp in a mixture of sambal oelek, honey, soy sauce, a little bit of lime juice and topped the finished tacos with a bright and crunchy daikon radish slaw for a fresh bite. If you like spicy food, you're going to love these tacos!

INSTRUCTIONS

Marinate the shrimp: In a large bowl, whisk together the sambal oelek, honey, soy sauce, sesame oil, lime juice, green onions, cilantro, and garlic. Mix in the shrimp, making sure they are completely submerged and evenly coated in the marinade. Marinate in the refrigerator for 30 minutes.

Meanwhile, preheat the oven to 400°F (200°C). Line a baking sheet with foil.

Arrange the shrimp on the baking sheet, add a spoonful of the marinade on top of each shrimp, and roast until cooked through, 8 to 9 minutes.

Make the slaw: In a medium bowl, toss together the daikon radish, carrot, cilantro, and lime juice. Season with salt to taste.

To assemble: Place a few shrimp on a warm tortilla, top with the slaw, and serve with lime wedges and avocado.

FOR THE MARINATED SHRIMP

4 tablespoons sambal oelek chili paste

3 tablespoons honey

2½ tablespoons reduced-sodium soy sauce

2½ tablespoons sesame oil

Juice of 1 lime

3 green onions, chopped

2 tablespoons chopped fresh cilantro

4 garlic cloves, minced

1 pound (455 g) 31–40 medium-large shrimp, peeled and deveined

FOR THE SLAW

1½ cups (160 g) julienned daikon radish

¾ cup (85 g) shredded peeled carrot

¼ cup (10 g) chopped fresh cilantro

1 tablespoon (½ ounce) fresh lime juice (from ½ lime)

¼ teaspoon Diamond Crystal kosher salt

FOR ASSEMBLY

Corn tortillas, warmed

Lime wedges

Avocado, sliced (optional)

Makes 4 tortas

4 portobello mushrooms

2 tablespoons olive oil

FOR THE DREDGE

1 cup (125 g) all-purpose flour

2 large eggs

1 tablespoon Valentina hot sauce (or your favorite hot sauce)

1½ cups (150 g) plain dried bread crumbs

1 teaspoon Diamond Crystal kosher salt

1 teaspoon granulated garlic

1 teaspoon granulated onion

FOR ASSEMBLY

¼ cup (60 ml) canola oil

Mayonnaise

4 telera rolls, halved and toasted

Lettuce leaves

Sliced tomato

Sliced avocado

Torta de Milanesa de Portobello

Having friends who follow different diets means recipes need to be adapted from time to time to ensure everyone you welcome into your home is able to enjoy good food. Although milanesa often refers to breaded and fried cuts of meat, this one is vegetarian friendly, using large portobello mushroom caps as the "protein."

INSTRUCTIONS

Preheat the oven to 400°F (200°C). Line a sheet pan with a wire cooling rack.

Prep the mushrooms by removing any stems and brushing the caps with the olive oil. Place the caps gill side down on the wire rack and roast for 20 minutes. This helps precook the mushrooms and get rid of any extra liquid for a better fry. Once the mushrooms have roasted, set them aside until they are cool enough to handle. (Hold onto the sheet pan and cooling rack.)

Make the dredge: Set up three shallow bowls (I use pie dishes) for a dredging station. Place the flour in one, beat the eggs with the hot sauce in the second, and place the bread crumbs in the third. Season both the flour and bread crumbs with ½ teaspoon each of the salt, garlic, and onion.

To assemble: In a medium skillet, heat the oil over medium heat. Lightly pat the mushroom caps dry with a paper towel. Working with one at a time, dip each cap into the flour to evenly coat both sides, then move on to the egg and do the same, making sure any extra egg drips off, then dip each side into the seasoned bread crumbs, pressing on the mushroom to make sure its entire surface is completely coated in bread crumbs.

Working in batches, fry the mushrooms until lightly golden brown, 1 to 2 minutes per side. Transfer to the cooling rack on the baking sheet you roasted them on to drain any excess oil.

To serve, spread mayonnaise on each half of a telera. Top with lettuce, a mushroom cap, tomato, avocado, and the top half of the roll.

Tacos Tuxpeños

TUXPAN TACOS

Serves 5 or 6

Tacos Tuxpeños, sometimes referred to as tacos de canasta (basket tacos) or tacos al vapor (steamed tacos), is a dish we had whenever mi mamá was feeling homesick. They reminded her of her childhood in Colima, enjoying these tacos during her lunch breaks at school con sus amigas. The taco Tuxpeño originated in the tiny pueblo of Tuxpan and became famous because the train from Colima would stop there and women would stand outside with baskets filled with tacos kept warm by their own steam, ready to feed hungry passengers. The taco consists of pork stewed in a guajillo-ancho broth until it shreds apart. I love the flavorful filling, but instead of warming these tacos in their own steam, I like to serve mine on a crispy fried tortilla.

INSTRUCTIONS

In a large pot, combine the guajillos, anchos, and enough water to completely submerge the chiles. Bring to a boil over high heat, then reduce the heat to low and simmer until the chiles have softened, about 15 minutes.

Use a slotted spoon to scoop out the chiles and transfer them to a blender. Add 2 cups (475 ml) of the chile cooking liquid to the blender (if you end up with less than that, add fresh water to make up the difference). Add the chicken stock, onion, garlic, thyme, cloves, cumin, and salt. Blend (be sure to open the steam vent/center cap and cover with a towel to avoid explosive hot liquid) on high speed for about 45 seconds to make sure it's fairly smooth.

Run the sauce through a fine-mesh sieve right into a slow cooker, 6-quart (6 liter) Dutch oven, or pressure cooker. Use a spoon to push the liquid through as needed. Stir in the bay leaves and add the pork.

In a slow cooker: Cover and cook on low for 6 to 8 hours, until the pork shreds easily. In a Dutch oven: Cover and cook over medium heat for 2 hours to 2 hours 30 minutes. In a pressure cooker: Cook at high pressure for 45 minutes, then quick-release the pressure.

(continued)

6 large guajillo chiles (about 5½ inches/14 cm long) (1½ ounces), stemmed and seeded

2 ancho chiles (1 ounce), stemmed and seeded

2 cups (475 ml) low-sodium chicken stock

¼ small yellow onion

5 garlic cloves, peeled

1 teaspoon fresh thyme leaves

2 whole cloves

¼ teaspoon ground cumin

1 tablespoon Diamond Crystal kosher salt, plus more to taste

2 bay leaves

3 pounds (1.35 kg) pork butt or pork shoulder, trimmed and cut into 4-inch (10 cm) cubes

FOR ASSEMBLY

Vegetable oil, for frying

24 mini corn tortillas (street taco size)

Diced onion

Chopped fresh cilantro

Sliced radishes

Salsa de Molcajete (page 27)

Lime wedges

FOR THE JALAPEÑO CREMA

1 cup (240 ml) crema Mexicana

2 tablespoons mayonnaise

2 tablespoons fresh lemon juice

¾ teaspoon garlic powder

½ teaspoon onion powder

¼ cup (60 g) chopped pickled jalapeños

FOR THE DRY DREDGE

½ cup (65 g) all-purpose flour

2 tablespoons cornstarch

FOR THE FISH

17 saltine crackers

⅔ cup (80 g) all-purpose flour

2 teaspoons kosher salt

1½ teaspoons New Mexico chile powder

1½ teaspoons granulated garlic

1½ teaspoons onion powder

1 teaspoon smoked paprika

½ teaspoon freshly ground black pepper

2 large eggs

12 ounces (355 ml) Mexican blonde lager, such as Corona or Modelo

Tacos de Pescado

Serves 4 or 5

FISH TACOS

I grew up in a typical Catholic home, where we observed Lent every spring. It meant we weren't allowed to eat meat on Fridays, but my siblings and I didn't really mind because we loved eating seafood; we would have eaten ceviche and mojarras fritas (whole deep-fried tilapia) every day if we could have. One of the many dishes mi mamá would prepare for us during this time were tacos de pescado. Her secret for a nice, crunchy crust was to crush up saltine crackers and incorporate them into the fish batter. I still use this technique for my own fish tacos, incorporating pulverized saltines into a flavorful Ensenada-style beer batter with garlic, New Mexico chiles, onion, and smoked paprika for a fish taco topped with a briny jalapeño crema.

INSTRUCTIONS

Make the jalapeño crema: In a medium bowl, whisk together the crema Mexicana, mayonnaise, lemon juice, garlic powder, and onion powder. Fold in the chopped jalapeño and let rest in the fridge until needed.

Prepare the dry dredge: In a shallow bowl, whisk together the flour and cornstarch and set aside.

Make the fish: In a food processor, pulse the saltines for about 30 seconds, or until completely fine and blitzed. In a large shallow bowl, whisk together the saltine cracker powder, flour, salt, chile powder, granulated garlic, onion powder, smoked paprika, and black pepper. Whisk in the eggs and beer until fully incorporated.

Line a wire cooling rack with paper towels. Pour 2 inches (5 cm) of oil into a 6-quart (6 liter) Dutch oven and heat to 375°F (190°C). While the oil heats, pat the fish fillets dry with a paper towel (the breading will not stick to the fish if wet).

(continued)

Platillos Fuertes

(MAIN DISHES)

Cuyutlàn (2016)

I've been finding myself in the kitchen con mi mamá more and more as I get older. The end-of-year holidays, especially, give me the opportunity to get to cook alongside her and learn some of her secrets that she learned from her mom and su abuelita, and we've both realized just how different each of us cooks. Mi mamá cooks with corazón, con pasión, and with guidance from an unknown magical force that whispers in her ear just how much salt to add, how long to simmer the frijoles for, and how many chiles de árbol to add to her salsa before it gets too spicy. I, on the other hand, tend to be more analytical: I need to understand an ingredient's purpose in a dish, I need to have exact measurements, and I need to make sure my dish is perfectly balanced. Mi mamá has been teaching me to trust my instincts, the same ones that I followed the first time I got in the kitchen and successfully made chiles rellenos, and I've been finding that the more I trust my hands, the more my dishes taste like home.

In this chapter, we'll be making platillos fuertes, or main dishes. These include things like my pozole rojo and my chicken con chochoyotes (dumplings), two stews that are perfect for a reminder of home on a chilly winter night. I also include a whole BBQ meal consisting of michelada-braised ribs (that don't require a grill!), deviled egg macaroni salad, and sweet masa corn muffins. If you like to meal prep, make a big batch of my chorizo-spiced meatballs and store them in the freezer to use throughout the week, and make a batch of my cilantro pesto, so you can cook a box of pasta and have a quick dinner. If you love seafood as much as I do, you'll enjoy my ceviche tostadas, my seared scallops served on pasta tossed in a creamy roasted poblano sauce, and the shrimp al mojo de ajo (shrimp cooked in a buttery garlic sauce).

Camarones a la Diabla

DEVILED SHRIMP

Camarones a la diabla, or deviled shrimp, get their name from the smoky and spicy chipotle sauce they are cooked in. The first time my mom made them at home, I remember falling in love with the sauce: It was sweet, it was tangy, and it was spicy all at the same time, and even though my face was beet red and drenched in sweat from the spiciness, I wanted more.

INSTRUCTIONS

In a medium saucepan, combine the guajillos, onion, garlic, and enough water to completely submerge the chiles. Bring to a boil over high heat, then reduce the heat to low and simmer until the chiles have softened, about 15 minutes.

Use a slotted spoon to transfer the chiles, onion, and garlic to a blender. Add 2¼ cups (530 ml) of the cooking liquid to the blender along with the tomato paste, vinegar, Worcestershire, chipotle pepper, oregano, paprika, vegetable oil, brown sugar, and salt. Blend (be sure to open the steam vent/center cap and cover with a towel to avoid explosive hot liquid) for 20 to 30 seconds until smooth.

Strain the sauce through a fine-mesh sieve into a deep skillet and bring to a simmer over medium heat. Simmer for 5 minutes, stirring occasionally. Stir in the shrimp, and cook for 10 to 12 minutes, until fully cooked. Taste for salt and adjust, then remove from heat. Serve with arroz blanco.

4 large guajillo chiles (about 5½ inches/14 cm long) (1 ounce), stemmed and seeded

¼ yellow onion

5 garlic cloves, peeled

1 (6 ounce/170 g) can tomato paste

2 tablespoons apple cider vinegar

1½ tablespoons Worcestershire sauce

1 chipotle pepper in adobo sauce

¾ teaspoon dried Mexican oregano

¼ teaspoon smoked paprika

½ tablespoon vegetable oil

1 tablespoon packed light brown sugar

1 teaspoon Diamond Crystal kosher salt, plus more to taste

2 pounds (910 g) 21–25 jumbo shrimp, deveined, shell on

Arroz Blanco (page 44), for serving

Serves 4 or 5

Camarones al Mojo de Ajo

SHRIMP IN GARLIC SAUCE

Camarones al mojo de ajo, a traditional Mexican dish similar to Italian shrimp scampi, have everything I love all in one dish: shrimp, butter, and tons of garlic! We start by melting the butter and infusing it with black pepper, lemon zest, and garlic. After we let it bloom for a bit, we add the shrimp with the shell on to make sure the sauce clings to every single crevice. Be sure to serve these shrimp with arroz blanco and a few dinner rolls, because this sauce will have you wanting to sop up every last drop!

¾ cup (1½ sticks/170 g) unsalted butter, at room temperature

1 teaspoon Diamond Crystal kosher salt

Grated zest of 1 lemon

½ teaspoon freshly ground black pepper

6 garlic cloves, finely minced

2 pounds (907 g) 21-25 jumbo shrimp, shell on and deveined

Arroz Blanco (page 44), for serving

Lemon wedges, for serving

Dinner rolls

INSTRUCTIONS

In a large skillet, melt the butter over low heat. Once the butter has melted and bubbles have begun to form, whisk in the salt, lemon zest, and black pepper and cook for 1 minute. Increase the heat to medium-low, add the garlic, and cook, stirring occasionally, for 3 minutes to infuse into the butter.

Add the shrimp and toss in the melted butter. Let them cook on one side for about 5 to 6 minutes, then flip and let cook until they turn completely pink in color, another 5 to 6 minutes, then remove from the heat. Taste for salt and adjust, then serve with arroz blanco, lemon wedges, and your favorite dinner rolls.

Pozole Blanco
WHITE POZOLE

Whenever there is a reason to celebrate, I can always count on my family to have a giant pot of pozole blanco simmering on the stove in wait. Pozole is a traditional stew made with hominy and pork, with onion and garlic as the base for the broth, topped with shredded cabbage, Mexican oregano, avocado, sea salt, and lime juice. There are different variations of pozole, like pozole rojo (red), pozole verde (green), and pozole seco (dry), which Colima is famously known for. The day after mi mamá made pozole blanco, she would make us pozole seco with the leftovers by heating up a tablespoon or two of lard and frying up the leftover pozole until the broth evaporated and the lightly crisped hominy would be left behind. It would be served in a bowl and topped with traditional pozole fixings!

INSTRUCTIONS

In a blender, combine the onion, garlic, 2 cups (475 ml) water, vinegar, salt, oregano, and thyme and blend until smooth.

In a 6 quart (6 liter) Dutch oven, melt the lard over medium heat. Add the pork and sear for 5 minutes on one side, then flip and sear for another 5 minutes. Pour in the blended mixture and use a silicone spatula to give it a stir and to loosen up any chunks of pork that might have stuck to the bottom.

Add 4 cups (1 liter) water and the hominy and its liquid. Give it one last stir and bring to a boil, then cover, reduce the heat to low, and cook the pozole until the pork shreds easily, 2 hours to 2 hours 30 minutes. Adjust the salt to taste.

To serve: Ladle the pozole into bowls and top with your favorite fixings like cabbage, radishes, and salsa roja. Add a sprinkle of sea salt and Mexican oregano and finish with a squeeze of lime.

½ medium yellow onion, roughly chopped

8 garlic cloves, peeled

1 teaspoon distilled white vinegar

2 teaspoons Diamond Crystal kosher salt, plus more to taste

½ teaspoon dried Mexican oregano, plus more for serving

½ teaspoon fresh thyme leaves

1½ teaspoons lard

2½ pounds (1137.5 g) pork shoulder, cut into 4-inch (10 cm) cubes

2 (29 ounce/822 g) cans white hominy, undrained

FOR SERVING

Shredded cabbage

Sliced radishes

Sea salt

Mexican oregano

Lime wedges

Salso roja

Pozole Rojo

RED POZOLE

Serves 5 to 7

Pozole rojo is my favorite pozole. It's usually made with chicken, and it gets its color from the different smoky red chiles added to the stock. Pozole rojo wasn't very common in our household, as my mom never made it for us growing up, so the only times we'd get to enjoy it was whenever it was served at a friend's pachanga (celebration), and I'd always be sure to eat as many bowls as I could possibly scarf down in one sitting.

INSTRUCTIONS

Make the stock: In a large soup pot or Dutch oven, heat the oil over medium-low heat. Add the onion and cook until it starts to turn translucent, about 5 minutes. Add the cilantro and add the head of garlic, cut sides down, and cook for 2 minutes. Add the thyme and bay leaves and cook for 2 more minutes. Pour in 6 cups (1.4 liters) water and sprinkle in the salt. Add the chicken thighs and bring to a simmer, cover, then reduce the heat to low and cook for 1 hour.

With a slotted spoon, remove the chicken. When cool enough to handle, shred the chicken with two forks and set aside.

Strain the stock into a large bowl and return it to the soup pot or Dutch oven. Add 4 cups (1 liter) water and the hominy with the liquid. Bring the mixture back up to a simmer and cook for 30 minutes.

Meanwhile, make the chile puree: In a medium saucepan, combine all the chiles with enough water to completely submerge them. Bring to a boil over high heat, then reduce the heat to low and simmer until the chiles have softened, about 15 minutes.

Use a slotted spoon to transfer the chiles to a blender along with ½ cup (120 ml) of the cooking liquid. Add the garlic, onion, cilantro, vinegar, oregano, cumin, and salt. Blend (be sure to open the steam vent/center cap and cover with a towel to avoid explosive hot liquid) for 20 to 30 seconds until smooth.

(continued)

FOR THE STOCK

1 tablespoon vegetable oil

½ white onion, chopped

½ cup (20 g) cilantro, leaves and stems

1 head garlic, sliced horizontally

2 sprigs fresh thyme

2 bay leaves

1 tablespoon Diamond Crystal kosher salt

4 pounds (1.35 kg) bone-in, skin-on chicken thighs

2 (29 ounce/822 g) cans hominy, undrained

FOR THE CHILE PUREE

5 large guajillo chiles (about 5½ inches/14 cm long) (about 1¼ ounces), stemmed and seeded

3 ancho chiles (about 1½ ounces), stemmed and seeded

2 to 3 chiles de árbol (use 2 if you'd like less heat)

4 garlic cloves, peeled

¼ cup chopped white onion

¼ cup (10 g) chopped fresh cilantro leaves

2 teaspoons distilled white vinegar

1 teaspoon dried Mexican oregano

¼ teaspoon ground cumin

Makes
1 cup
(240 ml)

2½ cups (100 g) fresh cilantro, stems and leaves

1 cup (40 g) fresh basil leaves

5 garlic cloves, peeled

¼ cup (30 g) chopped walnuts

⅓ cup (3 ounces/85 grams) grated Cotija cheese

Zest from 1 lemon

¼ teaspoon crushed red pepper flakes

¼ teaspoon dried Mexican oregano

2 tablespoons fresh lemon juice

½ cup plus 2 tablespoons (150 ml) extra virgin olive oil

Diamond Crystal kosher salt

Cilantro Pesto

INSTRUCTIONS

In a food processor, combine half of the cilantro and all of the basil, garlic, walnuts, Cotija, lemon zest, pepper flakes, and oregano. Pulse a few times until everything is coarsely minced, then add the rest of the cilantro and the lemon juice and pulse a few more times until everything is finely minced.

Pour in the olive oil and pulse 3 or 4 times, just until everything is thoroughly combined. Scrape the pesto into a bowl and add salt to taste.

Pesto will keep for 3 to 4 days in a sealed container in the refrigerator. You can also store the pesto in a freezer-friendly container for up to 3 months, if stored properly.

Michelada Ribs

Ribs are one of the dishes that my parents ask me to make the most whenever I host family dinners. My parents loved going to BBQ joints for birthdays, and after spending hundreds year after year on dry mac and cheese and ribs with very little to no meat, I decided to make everything myself for half the cost. I like to braise the ribs in a mixture reminiscent of the flavors of a michelada—beer, Clamato, Worcestershire sauce—and braising them makes them really juicy and tender so the cooked meat just falls off the bone. I love deviled eggs, so along with the ribs I like to serve a creamy deviled egg macaroni salad, the cheesiest rajas con mac and cheese (mac and cheese with diced jalapeño and poblano chiles), and sweet and buttery corn bread muffins made with a mixture of cornmeal and masa harina to enhance the flavor of the corn. Recipes for those favorites follow so you can easily make your own BBQ-style dinner at home!

INSTRUCTIONS

Position racks in the top and bottom thirds of the oven and preheat the oven to 250°F (120°C).

Break the ribs down into four 1-pound (455 g) racks to ensure they cook evenly. Place a large piece of foil on top of a baking sheet without tucking in the edges. Place one of the slabs of ribs on the foil, sprinkle on 1 tablespoon of the steak seasoning, and use your hands to pat it into the meat. Seal up the ribs in an individual foil packet, leaving one end open to pour in the braising liquid. Repeat this process with the remaining slabs of ribs.

In a large measuring cup, whisk together the beer, Clamato juice, Worcestershire, soy sauce, and sugar to make a braising liquid.

Dividing evenly, pour the braising liquid into the open end of each one of the rib packets, then seal them completely. Arrange the ribs on two baking sheets.

Braise the ribs in the oven for 2 hours 45 minutes, switching the baking sheets from rack to rack at the 1½-hour mark.

(continued)

Serves 5 or 6

4 pounds (1.8 kg) pork baby back ribs (avoid spare ribs)

4 tablespoons steak seasoning (page 97)

12 ounces (355 ml) pilsner beer, such as Modelo Especial or Corona

½ cup (120 ml) Clamato juice

¼ cup (60 ml) Worcestershire sauce

1 tablespoon reduced-sodium soy sauce

1 teaspoon sugar

2½ cups (590 ml) Hibiscus BBQ Sauce (page 49)

FOR SERVING

Sweet Masa Corn Bread Muffins (recipe follows)

Deviled Egg Macaroni Salad (recipe follows)

Rajas con Mac and Cheese (recipe follows)

Remove the baking sheets from the oven and turn the broiler to high. Drain the braising liquid, discard the foil, and place the ribs back onto your pan. (If your broiler is small, you'll have to slice your racks in half and work in batches.) Brush some BBQ sauce onto both sides of the ribs and broil until the sauce caramelizes, about 4 minutes. Remove from the oven, brush on more of the BBQ sauce, and broil for another 4 minutes for the sauce to finish caramelizing, then remove and brush on a generous third coat. Repeat with the remaining slabs of ribs.

To serve: Let the ribs cool for a few minutes, then cut into individual-sized portions and serve with extra BBQ sauce on the side. Accompany the ribs with the muffins, macaroni salad, and mac and cheese.

Sweet Masa Corn Bread Muffins

INSTRUCTIONS

1 cup (125 g) all-purpose flour

¾ cup (90 g) masa harina

½ cup (60 g) cornmeal

¾ cup (150 g) sugar

2 teaspoons baking powder

1 teaspoon baking soda

1 teaspoon Diamond Crystal kosher salt

8 tablespoons (113 g) unsalted butter, melted and slightly cooled

2 tablespoons (75 ml) neutral oil, like canola or grapeseed

2 large eggs

1⅔ cups (394 ml) buttermilk

Preheat the oven to 350°F (180°C). Grease 18 cups of two standard muffin tins. If you're worried about your muffins releasing easily, line the cups with cupcake liners instead of greasing them.

In a large bowl, whisk together the flour, masa harina, cornmeal, sugar, baking powder, baking soda, and salt.

In another bowl, whisk together the melted butter, oil, and eggs until combined, then add the buttermilk and whisk just until it comes together. Add the buttermilk mixture to the flour mixture and whisk just until combined, making sure to not overmix.

Divide the batter evenly among the 18 muffin cups, filling them about three-quarters of the way (see Tip). Bake just until a toothpick inserted in a muffin comes out clean, 18 to 20 minutes, making sure not to overbake.

Place the pans on a wire cooling rack to cool for 5 minutes, then flip the pans over to pop the muffins out of the tins onto the rack. (If you're using cupcake liners, then you can just carefully remove them from the pans after 15 to 20 minutes.)

Serve the muffins warm or let them cool and store covered on the counter for up to 2 days.

Tip: It's about 3 tablespoons batter per muffin cup, so I like to use a medium cookie scoop, which is 1½ tablespoons, and do 2 scoops per muffin.

Makes
18 muffins

Deviled Egg Macaroni Salad

INSTRUCTIONS

Bring a large pot of well-salted water to a boil. Drop in the pasta and cook according to the package directions. Drain and rinse with cold water to stop the cooking and help cool it down. Set aside.

Peel the hard-boiled eggs and separate the yolks from the whites. In a large bowl, stir together the sour cream, mayonnaise, pickled jalapeño juice, mustard, salt, black pepper, and paprika. Place the yolks from the hard-boiled eggs in a fine-mesh sieve and push them through into the bowl to break them down and make them fluffy and fine. (If your mesh sieve is too fine, you might run into issues pushing them through. If this is the case, then just mash them up with a fork.) Mix the fluffy yolks into the sour cream mixture.

Roughly chop up the egg whites and add them along with the celery, green onions, jalapeños, olives, dill, and cooled pasta and mix well. The pasta salad tastes best when it rests for a couple of hours in the fridge prior to serving. Just cover the whole bowl with plastic wrap and refrigerate until you're ready to serve.

Right before you serve, adjust the salt to taste. Garnish with paprika and dill sprigs.

(continued)

Serves 6 to 8

Salt

1 pound (455 g) short pasta of your choice (I like to use cavatappi)

6 large eggs, hard-boiled

¾ cup (175 ml) sour cream or full-fat plain Greek yogurt

¾ cup (175 ml) mayonnaise

⅓ cup (75 ml) juice from a jar of pickled jalapeños

1½ tablespoons yellow mustard

1½ teaspoons Diamond Crystal kosher salt

½ teaspoon freshly ground black pepper

¼ teaspoon paprika, plus more for garnish

1 cup (100 g) chopped celery (3 to 4 stalks)

½ cup (30 g) thinly sliced green onions (3 to 4 onions)

2 tablespoons finely chopped pickled jalapeños

½ cup (80 g) chopped black olives

2 tablespoons finely chopped fresh dill, plus sprigs for garnish

Make the sopes: Divide the masa dough into about 25 tablespoon-sized balls using a measuring spoon. Use your hands to roll the masa into smooth balls, then place them in a bowl and cover them with a damp towel.

Line a baking sheet with a kitchen towel. Place a large skillet or comal over medium-low heat. Grab a ball of dough and place it on a tortilla press lined with plastic wrap or wax paper. Gently press down on the dough, until you have a disc 3½ inches (7.5 cm) in diameter. Peel the masa disc off onto your hand and place it in the preheated skillet. Cook the disc for 1 minute 30 seconds, then flip, and cook for an additional 2 minutes. Transfer the fried sopes to the paper towel to drain.

Remove the disc from the skillet and place it on a flat surface. Use your fingers to gently pinch the outside edge of the sope up to form a ¼-inch (6 mm) wall around the perimeter, working quickly while it is still hot. If you overcooked the sope, you won't be able to pinch the edges up. Place the sope on the kitchen towel to absorb condensation. Repeat the process with the remaining masa balls.

Line a plate with paper towels. In the same skillet, heat ¼ inch (6 mm) vegetable oil over medium heat. If your tomato sauce has cooled, heat it back up over medium-low heat while the sopes fry. Working in batches of 4 or 5, fry the sopes until they are golden brown, 2 to 3 minutes. Flip and cook for an additional 2 minutes. Transfer the fried sopes to the paper towels to drain.

To serve: Place 5 or 6 sopes on each plate and add 2 to 3 tablespoons ground beef on top of each sope. Use a ladle to pour some of the tomato broth over each sope, then top them with lettuce, radish, and finish by sprinkling Cotija over all the sopes. Serve with your favorite hot sauce.

Makes 40 meatballs

Chorizo-Spiced Meatballs

4 large guajillo chiles
(about 5½ inches/14 cm
long) (1 ounce), stemmed
and seeded

1 ancho chile (½ ounce),
stemmed and seeded plus
⅓ cup (78 ml) chile soaking
liquid

¼ white onion

5 garlic cloves, peeled

2 teaspoons apple cider
vinegar

1 teaspoon dried Mexican
oregano

1 teaspoon granulated onion

½ teaspoon smoked paprika

¼ teaspoon ground cumin

¼ teaspoon freshly
ground black pepper

⅛ teaspoon ground cloves

¼ teaspoon ground cinnamon

2 pounds (910 g) ground
chicken or turkey

2½ teaspoons Diamond
Crystal kosher salt

⅔ cup (3 ounces/85 g)
finely crumbled queso fresco

1 tablespoon minced
fresh cilantro

1½ cups (70 g) fresh
bread crumbs

1 large egg

This meatball recipe is a great staple for any kitchen. It contains an adobo that tastes just like chorizo, which shines with just about any protein. If you have a week when you need to meal prep or know you might not have much time to make dinner, you can make a full batch of these ahead of time and store them in the freezer (see Tip) and use them as you need them. If you keep a box of pasta and jar of your favorite sauce in your pantry, dinner comes together in less than an hour!

INSTRUCTIONS

In a medium saucepan, combine the guajillos, ancho, onion, garlic, and enough water to completely submerge the chiles. Bring to a boil over high heat, then reduce the heat to low and simmer until the chiles have softened, about 15 minutes.

With a slotted spoon, transfer the chiles, onion, and garlic to a blender. Add ⅓ cup (78 ml) of the cooking liquid, apple cider vinegar, the oregano, granulated onion, smoked paprika, cumin, black pepper, cloves, and cinnamon. Blend until smooth, 20 to 30 seconds.

In a large bowl, combine the ground chicken, salt, queso fresco, cilantro, bread crumbs, and egg. Use your hands to mix everything together. Once everything has been fully incorporated, pour in the blended guajillo mixture and use your hands to mix everything in once more.

Preheat the oven to 375°F (190°C). Line a large baking sheet with parchment paper.

Use a medium cookie scoop to scoop out and form the meatballs, then evenly space them out on the baking sheet. Bake until golden brown and the internal temperature is 165°F (74°C), 22 to 25 minutes. If serving with pasta, let the meatballs simmer in your favorite pasta sauce for 10 minutes before serving.

Tip: To freeze, let the baked meatballs cool completely, then place in a freezer bag. They will keep in the freezer for up to 1 month if stored properly. To reheat: Simmer for 15 to 20 minutes in your favorite pasta sauce until fully warmed through.

Tostadas de Camarón

SHRIMP CEVICHE TOSTADAS

Serves 6 or 8

Whenever I think of the ocean, I start to miss mis abuelitos. I think about the stories mi abuelito Rogelio would share of his back-breaking days as a salinero in Cuyutlán, mining sea salt in the blazing sun every spring, and the festivities that would take place during Lent when the harvest was finished. Every time I pay them a visit, no trip is complete without heading to Cuyutlán for the day to sit in front of the ocean and enjoy a nice bowl of ceviche con la familia. My ceviche de camarón is a mixture of diced tomato, cucumber, onion, and chopped cilantro. I like to keep mine simple with shredded imitation crabmeat and a combination of cooked shrimp and lime-cooked shrimp, accompanied by an ice-cold Negra Modelo.

INSTRUCTIONS

Make the ceviche: Set up a large bowl of ice and water. In a medium saucepan, bring 5 cups (1.2 liters) water to a boil over high heat. Add 1 pound (455 g) of the shrimp and cook until they turn completely pink, 3 to 4 minutes. Use a slotted spoon to immediately transfer the shrimp to the ice bath to stop them from cooking. (Letting them cook any longer will result in rubbery, overcooked shrimp.)

In a medium bowl, combine the remaining 1 pound (455 g) shrimp and the lime juice, making sure all of the shrimp are completely submerged. Cover the bowl with plastic wrap and place in the fridge. Let the shrimp "cook" in the lime juice until they are completely pink in color, 15 to 20 minutes. Drain the shrimp.

In a large bowl, toss together the tomatoes, cucumber, red onion, cilantro, and shredded imitation crab and sliced serrano. Fold in the lime-cooked shrimp and the parboiled shrimp.

Make the seasoning: In a small bowl, whisk together the lime juice, celery salt, granulated garlic, and black pepper. Pour the seasoning over the ceviche toss everything together once more, then taste for salt and adjust.

To serve: Top a tostada with 1 cup (200 g) to 1½ cups (300 g) of the ceviche. Top the ceviche with avocado and finish with a sprinkle of sea salt. Serve with lime wedges and hot sauce.

FOR THE CEVICHE

2 pounds (907 g) 21-25 medium shrimp, peeled, deveined, and halved lengthwise through the back

1½ cups (355 ml) lime juice (10 to 12 limes)

2 pounds (907 g) Roma (plum) tomatoes, diced

2 cucumbers, peeled and diced

½ cup (60 g) very thinly sliced red onion

½ cup (20 g) chopped fresh cilantro

1 cup (135 g) shredded imitation crab

1 serrano pepper, thinly sliced, or diced

FOR THE SEASONING

Juice of 2 limes

1¼ teaspoons celery salt

½ teaspoon freshly ground black pepper

½ teaspoon granulated garlic

Diamond crystal kosher salt to taste

FOR SERVING

Tostadas

Sliced avocado

Sea salt

Key lime halves

Valentina or Tapatío hot sauce

Chicken con Chochoyotes

Serves 5 or 6

CHICKEN AND MASA DUMPLINGS

When I was thinking of what my version of chicken and dumplings would look like, I immediately thought of caldo de pollo, a comforting chicken stew mi mamá would make on cold winter days, and chochoyotes, Mexico's answer to the dumpling. Chochoyotes are these little round balls of corn masa with a crater in the middle that are typically cooked in brothy soups—a match made in heaven.

INSTRUCTIONS

Make the soup: In a large pot or Dutch oven, melt the butter over medium heat. Add the onion, carrots, and celery and cook until softened, 5 to 7 minutes. Add the garlic and cook for a minute until fragrant, then add the thyme sprigs, cilantro, kosher salt, pepper, celery salt, oregano, and 8 cups (1.9 liters) water and stir to combine. Add the chicken thighs, bring the soup to a simmer, and cook uncovered for 30 minutes.

Meanwhile, make the chochoyotes: In a bowl, use your hands to combine the masa, 1 cup (240 ml) water, lard, and salt. Break off 25 tablespoon-sized pieces and roll them into balls. Carefully use your finger to make a crater in the center of each to ensure they cook evenly, then set aside and cover with a damp towel until you're ready to cook them.

After the soup has been cooking for 30 minutes, remove the chicken and thyme sprigs and reduce the heat under the soup to the lowest simmer possible. Add the chochoyotes, making sure they're fully submerged in the broth, and cook gently for 20 minutes. They should puff up slightly but not change too much in appearance.

When the chicken is cool enough to handle, remove it from the bone and shred.

Once the dumplings are cooked, add the shredded chicken to the pot along with the peas and cook for an additional 5 minutes. Adjust the salt to taste and serve.

FOR THE SOUP

4 tablespoons (60 g) unsalted butter

1 large yellow onion, chopped

1 cup (120 g) sliced carrots (about 2 large)

1 cup (100 g) chopped celery (about 2 stalks)

5 garlic cloves, minced

3 sprigs fresh thyme

3 tablespoons minced fresh cilantro

1 tablespoon Diamond Crystal kosher salt, plus more to taste

1 teaspoon freshly ground black pepper

½ teaspoon celery salt

½ teaspoon dried Mexican oregano

4 bone-in, skin-on chicken thighs (about 2 pounds/ 910 g total)

1 cup (135 g) frozen peas

FOR THE CHOCHOYOTES

1¾ cups (220 g) masa harina

2 tablespoons lard

1½ teaspoons Diamond Crystal kosher salt

Serves 4 or 6

Roasted Garlic and Poblano Pasta with Seared Scallops

FOR THE SAUCE

5 poblano chiles, 4½ ounces (115 g) each

6 garlic cloves, unpeeled

⅓ cup, plus 1 tablespoon 55 ml) extra virgin olive oil

⅓ cup (40 ml) sour cream

⅔ cup (3 ounces/85 g) queso fresco

¼ cup (10 g) cilantro leaves

1 teaspoon Diamond Crystal kosher salt, plus more to taste

¼ teaspoon freshly ground black pepper

FOR THE SCALLOPS

12 ounces (340 g) scallops

1 tablespoon vegetable oil

Diamond Crystal kosher salt and freshly ground black pepper, plus more for serving

1 pound (455 g) pasta (I use tagliatelle)

FOR SERVING

Freshly ground black pepper or red pepper flakes

Grated Cotija or Parmesan cheese

A few years ago, my friend Thelma introduced me to her mom's recipe for espagueti verde, a dish popular in Mexico composed of spaghetti tossed in a creamy roasted poblano sauce that's typically enjoyed as a side dish. I liked her recipe so much that I started making it often for myself, and it soon began to evolve based on whatever I had in my fridge that night. It eventually became a cross between espagueti verde and Peruvian tallarines verdes. I found that seared scallops paired perfectly with this sauce, and my version of it has both roasted garlic and roasted poblanos with creamy queso fresco. I like using tagliatelle and cavatappi (corkscrew pasta) for this, but feel free to substitute with your favorite pasta!

INSTRUCTIONS

Make the sauce: Preheat the oven to 400°F (200°C). Halve the chiles, then remove the stems and seeds. Place the poblanos skin side up with the unpeeled garlic on a baking sheet. Drizzle 1 tablespoon of the olive oil over the poblanos, then roast in the oven for 20 minutes.

Remove from the oven. Place the poblanos in a bowl, then seal with plastic wrap, and let the chiles steam for about 10 minutes. Once the poblanos are cool, use your fingers to remove the waxy outer skin and then the stem and seeds. Peel the garlic cloves and add them to a blender, along with the poblanos, the remaining olive oil, the sour cream, crumbled queso fresco, cilantro leaves, salt, and pepper. Blend until smooth, then taste and adjust for salt.

Make the scallops: Pat the scallops completely dry with a paper towel. If the scallops still have their side muscle on, remove and discard.

In a large skillet, heat the vegetable oil over medium heat until sizzling. Season the tops of the scallops with salt and pepper, then

(continued)

PRESSURE COOKER BIRRIA

Make the adobo sauce through blending until smooth.

Pour the adobo sauce into the pressure cooker. Add the beef and bay leaf and pour in 8 cups (1.9 liters) water and give it a stir. Cook on high pressure for 50 minutes. Let the pressure release naturally for 10 minutes, then quick-release the remaining pressure. Serve as above.

Postres

✳ (DESSERTS) ✳

Cancún (2015)

I'm so excited to finally get to this chapter because we're focusing on desserts! When I was in high school and still lived with my parents, there were a few desserts I dared to try to whip up. All, of course, were from a box mix. I'd run to the store across the street and grab a box of strawberry cake mix, brownies, flan, and these Oreo cheesecake bars my mom fell in love with that she asks me about every so often. When I was thinking about the different desserts I had enjoyed as a kid, I realized it was mostly cake and gelatinas (flavored gelatin desserts), but I wanted to make them a little more exciting than what we used to have then. In my interpretations of these beloved childhood treats, I took inspiration from the flavor profiles of different aguas frescas, cult candies, and even coffee. If you have a big sweet tooth just as I do, you're about to be in for a real treat!

Duvalín Jello

Serves
16 to 20

This gelatina was inspired by the Duvalín, a Mexican cream candy I grew up with that had the texture of store-bought frosting. Most of us would ditch the little plastic paddle it came with to scoop out the cream with our fingers. It came in a variety of flavor combinations—vanilla and hazelnut, hazelnut and strawberry, vanilla and strawberry—but the ultimate stroke of luck was when you got one with all three flavors. So I made this gelatina to guarantee I'd always be able to enjoy all three in one bite.

INSTRUCTIONS

In a small bowl, combine the gelatin and 1 cup (240 ml) water and set aside for about 5 minutes so the gelatin can bloom. Coat a 10-cup (2.5 liter) Bundt pan or jello mold lightly with cooking spray and set aside.

Make the strawberry layer: In a blender, combine the strawberries, half-and-half, and sugar and blend on high until the mixture is smooth, 20 to 30 seconds. Strain the mixture through a fine-mesh sieve into a 2-quart (2 liter) saucepan. Warm slightly over medium heat—you want to warm up the mixture just enough to melt the gelatin, but not enough to boil and curdle the mixture. Once warm, reduce the heat to low, and add about one-third of the bloomed gelatin (it should be like a big chunk of an eraser after it's bloomed). Stir occasionally until the gelatin has dissolved. To make this layer pinker, whisk in a drop or two of red gel food coloring.

Pour the strawberry gelatin mixture layer into the Bundt pan or mold. Place the pan in the fridge to set for 1 hour to 1 hour 30 minutes. Rinse out the saucepan to have it ready for the next layer.

Make the vanilla layer: After the strawberry layer has been setting for 1 hour, in the saucepan combine the half-and-half, sugar, and cinnamon stick and heat over low heat to just under a simmer. Remove from the heat and let the mixture sit for 20 minutes to let the cinnamon stick steep, then use a slotted spoon to remove it. Rewarm slightly over medium heat, reduce the heat to low, then add half of the remaining bloomed gelatin and stir until it's dissolved. Stir in the vanilla extract, remove from the heat, and let cool to room temperature, about 15 minutes, so it does not melt the strawberry layer.

(continued)

Ingredients

4 tablespoons unflavored gelatin from about 6 packets

FOR THE STRAWBERRY LAYER

8 ounces (225 g) strawberries, hulled

1 cup (240 ml) half-and-half

⅔ cup (134 g) sugar

Red gel food coloring (optional)

FOR THE VANILLA LAYER

2 cups (480 ml) half-and-half

¾ cup (150 g) sugar

1 (4-inch/10 cm) stick Mexican cinnamon, broken in half

1 teaspoon vanilla extract

FOR THE CHOCOLATE HAZELNUT LAYER

2 cups (480 ml) half-and-half

⅔ cup (165 ml) Nutella

Carefully pour the room-temperature vanilla layer into the Bundt pan or mold over the strawberry layer and return to the refrigerator for 1 hour to 1 hour 30 minutes. Rinse out the saucepan to have it ready for the next layer.

Make the chocolate layer: After the two layers have been setting for 1 hour, in a saucepan, bring the half-and-half to just under a simmer over low heat. Add the Nutella and whisk until it melts and resembles hot chocolate. Add the final bit of the bloomed gelatin and stir until the gelatin has dissolved. Remove from the heat and let cool to room temperature, about 15 minutes, so it does not melt the other layers.

Carefully pour the room-temperature chocolate layer into the Bundt pan or mold over the vanilla layer and return it to the refrigerator for 1 hour 30 minutes to 2 hours.

When you're ready to serve, use your fingertips to carefully pull the gelatin away from the edge of the pan, or run a thin knife along the perimeter and invert the dessert onto a serving platter.

Cafe de Olla Flan

CINNAMON COFFEE CUSTARD

There's a little restaurant in the pueblito de Suchitlán called Los Portales de Suchitlán where I love to have breakfast whenever I'm visiting mis abuelitos. One of the things this area of Colima is known for is coffee, and this gorgeous open-air restaurant in the middle of the jungle-like forest has coffee trees growing right next to your table! Whenever I go, I love having cafe de olla with my breakfast. If you're not familiar, cafe de olla is the way many people in Mexico enjoy coffee. It is a very aromatic coffee made in an olla de barro (clay pot). The coffee is steeped with cinnamon and orange zest, and then sweetened with piloncillo, an unrefined cane sugar. This flan has all of the components of cafe de olla: The custard base steeps with coffee and cinnamon, and then a caramel is made with sugar, orange juice, and orange zest, for a flan that is nice and creamy and packed with a cinnamon-coffee flavor.

INSTRUCTIONS

Preheat the oven to 300°F (148°C). Coat an 8-inch (20 cm) round cake pan with cooking spray.

Make the caramel: In a medium saucepan (make sure to use a saucepan that doesn't have a dark bottom so you can see the caramel change color), combine the orange juice and granulated sugar and stir over low heat with a silicone spatula just until everything has been combined. Add the orange zest. Increase the heat to medium and cook until this mixture is amber in color, occasionally swirling the pan, 8 to 12 minutes. As soon as it starts to turn amber in color, remove the orange zest with a slotted spoon, then remove the pan from the heat and pour the caramel into the cake pan. Holding the cake pan with a kitchen towel or oven mitt (the caramel will make the pan very hot), swirl the mixture around to make sure the bottom of the pan is evenly coated in caramel.

Make the flan: In a medium saucepan, combine the half-and-half and condensed milk and whisk over medium-low heat. Once the condensed milk has dissolved, stir in the cinnamon sticks, smashed

(continued)

FOR THE CARAMEL

3 tablespoons orange juice

⅔ cup (135 g) granulated sugar

3 (3 inch/7.5 cm) strips orange zest

FOR THE FLAN

2 cups (475 ml) half-and-half

1 (14 ounce/396 g) can sweetened condensed milk

2 (4-inch/10 cm) sticks Mexican cinnamon, broken in half

½ cup (65 g) medium-roast coffee beans, placed in a plastic bag, then smashed or broken up into smaller pieces with a kitchen mallet

Pinch of Diamond Crystal kosher salt

3 large eggs

1 teaspoon vanilla extract

(continued)

**1½ cups (355 ml) heavy
(whipping) cream**

1 teaspoon vanilla extract

**¼ cup (30 g) powdered
sugar**

**Grated orange zest,
for garnish**

coffee beans, and salt. Let the mixture come to a simmer, then remove it from the heat, cover, and let the mixture steep for 30 minutes.

Strain the milk-coffee mixture into the blender then add the eggs and vanilla extract and blend for 20 seconds, until smooth. Pour this mixture into the caramel-lined cake pan.

Place the cake pan in a bigger, shallow baking dish and fill the dish with water to come halfway up the sides of the cake pan. Loosely cover the flan with a sheet of foil lightly sprayed with nonstick spray and bake until the outer rim of the custard stays firm and the center jiggles a little, 1 hour 10 minutes to 1 hour 20 minutes. Check for doneness at the hour mark.

Remove the cake pan from the water bath and let cool on a wire cooling rack for about 30 minutes. Refrigerate for at least 4 hours to set before serving.

Once you are ready to serve, gently run a thin and sharp knife along the edge of the flan, then place a plate on top of the flan and invert.

Make the whipped topping: In a stand mixer fitted with the whisk attachment, combine the cream and vanilla extract, then sift in the powdered sugar. Turn the mixer to low, slowly increasing the speed up to high. Whisk until you get fairly steep peaks, 2 to 3 minutes.

Serve the flan with a dollop of the whipped cream and garnish with orange zest.

Tip: I highly recommend using an oven thermometer to make sure your oven is always heating up to the right temperature.

Serves 16 to 20

3 (6 ounce) packages flavored gelatin dessert of your choice (I used cherry, blue raspberry, and lemon)

6 cups (1.4 liters) boiling water

4 tablespoons unflavored gelatin from about 6 packets

3 cups whole milk

1 (4-inch/10 cm) stick Mexican cinnamon, broken in half

1 (14 ounce/396 g) can sweetened condensed milk

2 cups (475 ml) half-and-half

1½ teaspoons vanilla extract

Gelatina de Mosaico

MOSAIC JELLO

Gelatina de mosaico was always a mystery to me as a kid. I'd see it on my way out of Sunday school as the town ladies would line up outside to sell tamales, champurrado (a chocolate-based drink with corn masa), and gelatinas, and was always intrigued as to how'd they get all those colorful cubes of gelatina in there. But now that I cook for a living, I've found out how easy it is to make what I thought was a tasty magic trick. This mosaic jello uses gelatina de leche as a base in which colorful cubes of three other gelatin flavors are suspended. If you're having a birthday party, use plastic cups instead of a baking dish for individually portioned treats!

INSTRUCTIONS

Lightly coat three 8-inch (20 cm) square pans and one 9 × 13-inch (23 × 33 cm) baking pan with cooking spray.

In three separate bowls, mix each package of flavored gelatin with 2 cups (475 ml) boiling water. Pour each into its own greased square pan. Refrigerate for 1 hour.

After the jellos have been in the fridge for 30 minutes, make the milk gelatin. In a 3-quart (3 liter) saucepan, mix the gelatin into 1 cup (240 ml) water. Set aside for about 5 minutes so the gelatin can bloom. Set the saucepan over medium-low heat and stir occasionally until the gelatin has dissolved. Add the whole milk and heat to just under a simmer. Add the cinnamon stick, remove from the heat, and let the mixture steep for 30 minutes.

Remove the cinnamon stick and whisk in the condensed milk, half-and-half, and vanilla extract. Set aside while you prep the colored gelatins.

Remove the colored gelatins from the refrigerator and cut each flavor into 1-inch (36 mm) cubes. Evenly spread out and mix each flavor in the 9 × 13-inch pan. Pour the milk jello over the cubes. Refrigerate until set and firm, 2 to 3 hours.

When you're ready to serve, invert the gelatina onto a cutting board, cut into 3- to 4-inch (7.5 to 10 cm) cubes, and place on a serving platter.

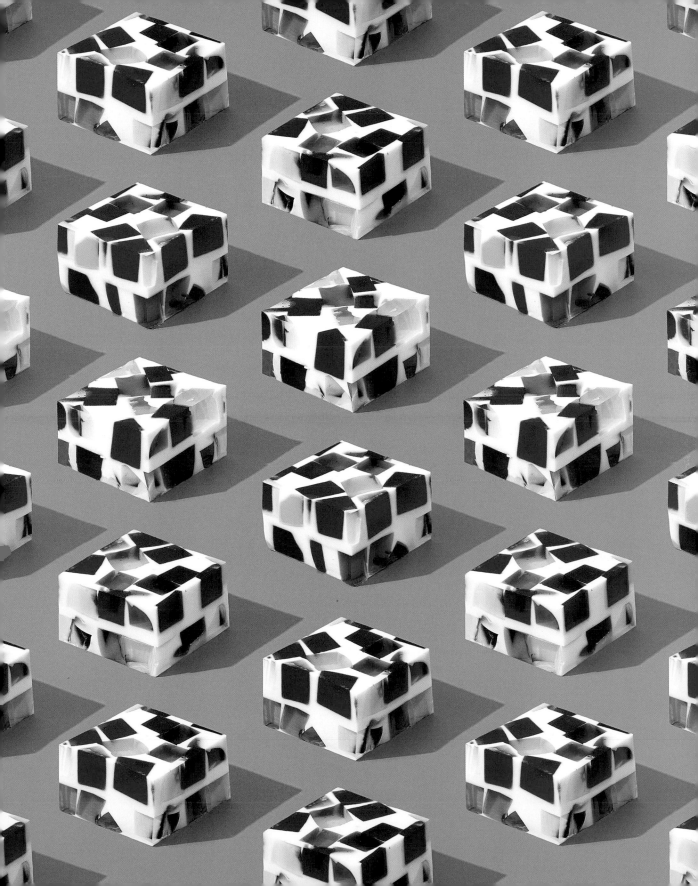

Strawberry Jamaica Cake

Serves 8 to 12

A few years ago, for my partner's birthday, I took him to visit Colima for the very first time. I was anxious to show him all of the different places I'd often talk about, and was excited for him to finally meet my grandparents and get to taste their amazing cooking. While we were there, I took him to el tianguis, or flea market, that has been setting up across from mi abuelita's house every Sunday since before I was born. We strolled up and down the different booths, stopping to look at the fresh produce, the fresh cuts of beef, and then we stumbled upon a booth with different aguas frescas that served combinations we had never had before. Our favorite was the strawberry jamaica (hibiscus), a combination I've wanted to use in a cake since tasting it.

INSTRUCTIONS

Make the cake: Preheat the oven to 350°F (180°C). Grease two 8-inch round cake pans and line the bottoms with rounds of parchment paper.

In a medium bowl, whisk together the flour, baking powder, and salt and set aside.

In a stand mixer fitted with the paddle attachment, beat the butter, oil, and the sugar on medium speed until light and fluffy and paler in color, about 2 minutes. Beat in the vanilla extract. Beat in the eggs, one at a time, making sure that each is mixed in before adding the next.

Add one-third of the flour mixture and mix on low to incorporate. Add one-third of the buttermilk, followed by another one-third of the flour mixture, another one-third of the buttermilk, and then finally the last amount of each. Mix just until combined, then use a rubber spatula to scrape down the sides of the bowl.

Divide the batter between the two pans and bake until a toothpick inserted comes out clean, 30 to 35 minutes. Then invert the cakes onto a cooling rack.

Make the hibiscus tea: In a heatproof bowl, combine the boiling water and hibiscus and let it steep for 15 minutes. Strain the tea into a measuring cup.

(continued)

FOR THE CAKE

2½ cups (315 g)
all-purpose flour

2½ teaspoons
baking powder

½ teaspoon Diamond
Crystal kosher salt

½ cup (1 stick/115 g)
unsalted butter,
at room temperature

2 tablespoons neutral oil
(like vegetable oil)

1¾ cups (350 g) sugar

1½ teaspoons
vanilla extract

3 large eggs

1⅓ cups (315 ml)
buttermilk

FOR THE
HIBISCUS TEA

2½ cups (625 ml)
boiling water

1¼ cups (44 g) dried
hibiscus flowers

FOR THE STRAWBERRY-
HIBISCUS FILLING

¼ cup (60 ml) hibiscus tea

1½ tablespoons cornstarch

¾ cups (1100 g)
**chopped strawberries
(from ¼ pound/112 g)**

¼ cup (50 g)
granulated sugar

1 tablespoon fresh
lime juice

FOR THE HIBISCUS
BUTTERCREAM

1⅔ cups (395 ml)
hibiscus tea

1⅔ cups (335 g)
granulated sugar

½ cup (65 g)
all-purpose flour

¼ teaspoon Diamond
Crystal kosher salt

3 sticks (340 g)
**unsalted butter,
at room temperature**

Make the strawberry-hibiscus filling: Transfer ¼ cup (60 ml) of the hibiscus tea to a 2-quart (2 liter) saucepan and let it cool to room temperature. Whisk in the cornstarch until combined, then add the strawberries, sugar, and lime juice. Set the pan over medium heat and cook, stirring occasionally, until the mixture starts to bubble and thicken, then continue cooking for 2 minutes. Transfer the filling to a bowl and place a piece of plastic wrap directly on the surface to prevent a skin from forming. Refrigerate the filling to cool completely.

Start the hibiscus buttercream: Transfer the remaining 1⅔ cups (395 ml) hibiscus tea to a 2-quart (2 liter) saucepan. Add the sugar and whisk to combine and dissolve. Sift the flour and salt into the saucepan, set the pan over medium heat, and cook, whisking occasionally, until the mixture starts to bubble. Reduce the heat to medium-low and cook for an additional 2 minutes. Transfer the hibiscus pudding to a large plate and press plastic wrap directly on the surface to prevent a skin from forming. Refrigerate to help it cool completely.

Once you're ready to assemble the cake, take the hibiscus pudding out of the refrigerator and let it sit for 30 minutes, to bring to room temperature. In a stand mixer fitted with the whisk attachment, beat the butter on medium speed until it becomes lighter in color and texture, about 1 minute. With the mixer on medium speed, add the hibiscus-pudding mixture 1 tablespoon at a time, until half the mixture has been added. Scrape down the sides of the bowl and repeat with the remainder of the hibiscus-flour mixture. Scrape down the sides and bottom of the bowl and turn the mixer to high. Beat the buttercream for 2 full minutes more, until light, smooth, and fluffy. If your hibiscus pudding happens to be cold when you go to add it to the butter, the butter will curdle up. Simply let the buttercream sit for 15 to 20 minutes, then whip it again.

To assemble the cake, place a layer of the vanilla cake on a cake stand or serving plate and spread a heaping ½ cup (120 ml) of the buttercream on top. Carefully spread all of the strawberry-hibiscus filling on top of the buttercream, then place the other layer of vanilla cake on top, placing it upside down so the top of the cake is level and flat. Use an offset spatula to evenly spread a thin layer of buttercream (the "crumb coat") all over the cake, filling in the gaps where the layers meet with frosting to make the outside of the cake smooth. Refrigerate for 30 minutes to firm up the crumb coat.

Finish frosting the outside of the cake with rest of the buttercream, making sure to beat it for a minute or so first, if the buttercream looks separated. Once the cake is frosted, store it in the fridge until ready to serve.

Champurrado Chocolate Sheet Cake

Serves 16 to 20

Champurrado is a drink—made with chocolate and milk and thickened with masa—that people in Mexico usually drink during Christmastime and when the weather starts to get a little colder. In Southern California, we'd buy it from the street vendors who would walk by every evening ringing their bells to let us know the tamales and champurrado had arrived. This moist chocolate sheet cake brings in the traditional champurrado flavors with the buttercream frosting.

INSTRUCTIONS

Make the chocolate cake: Preheat the oven to 350°F (180°C) then lightly grease a 9 by 13 inch (23 by 33 cm) baking pan.

Sift the cocoa powder into a large bowl, then whisk in the flour, sugar, baking soda, baking powder, salt, and ground cinnamon. In another bowl, whisk together the coffee, oil, buttermilk, and eggs. Add the cocoa mixture to the coffee mixture a little at a time, mixing just until combined.

Pour the batter into the pan and bake until a toothpick inserted comes out clean, 35 to 40 minutes. Set the cake on a wire cooling rack to cool completely for 30 to 40 minutes. If not assembling the cake right away, wrap the pan in plastic wrap and store in the fridge until ready.

Start the buttercream: In a 2-quart (2 liter) saucepan, mix together the sugar, chocolate, milk, and salt. Set over medium-low heat and bring to just below a simmer, stirring often to help dissolve the chocolate and sugar. Sift the flour, masa harina, and cocoa powder into the saucepan and increase the heat to medium. Whisk the mixture together and cook until it starts to bubble. Reduce the heat to medium-low and cook for an additional 2 minutes. Transfer the chocolate pudding mixture to a large plate and press plastic wrap directly on the surface to prevent a skin from forming. Refrigerate until cool.

(continued)

FOR THE CHOCOLATE CAKE

¾ cup (70 g) unsweetened cocoa powder

2½ cups (315 g) all-purpose flour

2 cups (400 g) sugar

1½ teaspoons baking soda

1 teaspoon baking powder

1 teaspoon Diamond Crystal kosher salt

1 teaspoon ground cinnamon

1 cup (200 ml) brewed coffee

½ cup (120 ml) neutral oil, such as grapeseed or canola

½ cup (120 ml) buttermilk

2 large eggs

(continued)

FOR THE CHAMPURRADO BUTTERCREAM

1¼ cups (250 g) sugar

½ cup (65 g) grated Mexican chocolate, such as Abuelita or Ibarra

1½ cups (355 ml) whole milk

¼ teaspoon Diamond Crystal kosher salt

¼ cup (30 g) all-purpose flour

¼ cup (30 g) masa harina

2 tablespoons cocoa powder

3 sticks (340 g) unsalted butter, at room temperature

Sprinkles

Once you're ready to assemble the cake, take the chocolate pudding mixture out of the refrigerator and let it sit for 30 minutes, to bring to room temperature. Beating the butter with the cold pudding mixture will curdle the butter and your frosting won't be smooth. If your butter curdles, just let it sit for 10 to 15 minutes, then beat it again.

In a stand mixer fitted with the whisk attachment, beat the butter on medium speed until lighter in color and texture, about 1 minute. With the mixer on medium speed, add the room temperature chocolate pudding mixture a tablespoon at a time, until half the mixture has been added. Scrape down the sides of the bowl and turn the mixer back to medium speed and repeat with the remainder of the chocolate pudding mixture. Scrape down the sides and bottom of the bowl and turn the mixer to high and beat the buttercream for 2 full minutes, until light, smooth, and fluffy.

To assemble the cake, spread the buttercream evenly over the cake, then top with your favorite sprinkles. Once the cake is frosted, store it in the fridge until ready to serve.

Guava Cheesecake Bars

Whenever family came back from visiting Mexico, they'd bring pan dulce, tortillas, and sweets with them as gifts. One of the sweets they always brought back was a guava paste roll that we'd cut chunks off and eat with a cold glass of milk whenever we were craving something sweet before bed. Guava paste is used in desserts like empanadas and pastelito pastries, and is sometimes served on crackers with cheese, which means it pairs exceptionally well with dairy. These cheesecake bars are creamy with a nice tang from the guava paste, but it's easy to swap out the guava for anything else you have in your pantry, like dulce de leche, if you're looking for a different flavor combination.

INSTRUCTIONS

Make the guava paste swirl: Roughly chop up the guava paste and place it in a small saucepan with ⅓ cup (80ml) water. Cook over low heat, stirring occasionally, until the guava paste melts. When the paste has almost completely melted, you can switch over to a whisk to stir and break down any lumps remaining. Set aside to cool slightly.

Preheat the oven to 350°F (180°C). Grease an 8-inch (20 cm) square baking pan and line it with parchment so two sides stick out to help you lift the bars out of the pan when baked.

Make the Maria cookie crust: In a food processor, combine the cookies, sugar, and salt and pulse for 15 to 20 seconds until the mixture resembles the texture of sand. Pour this mixture into a bowl, then pour in the melted butter and use a rubber spatula to fully incorporate the butter. Pour the crust mixture into the baking pan and use the bottom of a measuring cup to distribute it evenly, adding slight pressure to pack down the crust.

Make the cheesecake: In a stand mixer fitted with the paddle attachment, beat together the cream cheese, sugar, and vanilla extract on medium speed for a full minute to make sure the sugar is properly mixed in. Reduce the speed to the lowest setting and

(continued)

FOR THE GUAVA PASTE SWIRL

½ cup (3.75 ounces/ 100 g) guava paste

FOR THE MARIA COOKIE CRUST

1½ cups (180 g) Maria cookie crumbs (from about 35 cookies)

3 tablespoons sugar

⅛ teaspoon coarse salt

5 tablespoons (70 g) unsalted butter, melted

FOR THE CHEESECAKE

16 ounces (455 g) cream cheese

⅓ cup (65 g) sugar

½ teaspoon vanilla extract

2 large eggs

add the eggs, one at a time, making sure the first one is mixed in before adding the second. Scrape down the sides and bottom of the bowl, then give the mixer a 2- to 3-second burst on high speed to make sure everything is incorporated. Do not overmix—mixing the cheesecake batter as little as possible is key to making sure you don't whip too much air into it, causing it to inflate and then crack when baking.

Pour the cheesecake filling onto the crust, then spread evenly with an offset spatula. Dollop the guava onto the cheesecake evenly with a teaspoon, then use a sharp knife or skewer to swirl it into the cheesecake slowly, making sure not to cut deep enough to scratch the crust. Swirl from dollop to dollop to get the best effect.

Tap the pan on the counter to get rid of any hidden air bubbles and to smooth out the surface. Transfer to the oven and bake until the cheesecake is still just barely wobbly in the center and slightly puffed around the edges, 25 to 30 minutes. Remove from the oven and let cool at room temperature for 30 minutes before transferring to the fridge to cool completely.

When you're ready to serve, just lift the cheesecake out of the pan using the parchment sling, cut into 16 bars, and serve.

Churros with a Chocolate Dipping Sauce

The feelings and memories that the smell of fried dough tossed in cinnamon and sugar evoke in me are indescribable. It takes me back to trips across the border to Tijuana with mis tíos, sitting in the car eating churros watching street vendors zip in and out through the cars as we'd patiently wait to cross the border back to the US. It takes me back to la Feria de la Villa in Colima on a cool February night, walking around the fair enjoying the bright lights and carnival rides as a little kid with a bag of churros in hand. Churros are rather easy to make, and this recipe provides the basic framework so you can make them at home. Try substituting grated Abuelita chocolate in the dipping sauce or using mazapanes (a marzipan-like treat) in place of the cinnamon sugar for an easy twist on the classic churro flavors.

INSTRUCTIONS

In a medium saucepan, combine ¾ cup (175 ml) water, the milk, butter, and salt and cook over medium heat until the butter has melted and the mixture just begins to simmer.

Add the flour and stir until the mixture is combined and starts to form a ball. Cook for a minute or so more, until the dough firms up just a little bit more and starts to leave a slight film on the bottom of the pan. Transfer the dough to a large bowl and let cool for 5 to 6 minutes.

Add the eggs, one at a time, stirring very well to make sure each egg is mixed in before adding the next. Transfer the dough to a piping bag fitted with a Wilton 1M piping tip. Set the dough aside to rest while the oil heats up.

Pour 3 to 4 inches (7.5 to 10 cm) of vegetable oil into a large Dutch oven and heat to 360° to 375°F (182° to 190°C). In a wide shallow bowl, combine the sugar and cinnamon to create a cinnamon-sugar coating and set aside.

(continued)

Makes 30 to 40 churros

½ cup (120 ml) whole milk

8 tablespoons (115 g) unsalted butter

¼ teaspoon salt

1½ cups (190 g) all-purpose flour

4 large eggs

Vegetable oil, for deep-frying (about 6 cups/1.4 liters)

⅔ cup (135 g) granulated sugar

1 tablespoon ground cinnamon

1 cup (175 g) roughly chopped bittersweet chocolate

½ cup (120 ml) heavy (whipping) cream

Line a paper plate with paper towels. Pipe the churros out in 5- to 6-inch (12.4 to 15 cm) lengths and cut with a pair of scissors so they drop into the hot oil. Cook for 1 to 2 minutes on the first side, then flip and cook for 1 minute more. Transfer the churros to the paper towels to cool for about a minute, then toss in the cinnamon sugar.

In a small saucepan, gently heat the chocolate and cream together until the chocolate melts. Serve the dipping sauce alongside the churros.

MAZAPAN CHURROS

Substitute ⅓ cup (3oz/88 g) crumbled mazapanes (from 3 regular-sized mazapanes) plus ⅓ cup granulated sugar plus 1 teaspoon ground cinnamon for the cinnamon sugar. Serve the dipping sauce alongside the churros.

ABUELITA CHOCOLATE CHURROS

Substitute ⅔ cup (90 g) grated Abuelita chocolate plus 1 teaspoon ground cinnamon for the cinnamon sugar. Serve the dipping sauce alongside the churros.

Dulce de Leche Chocoflan

Chocoflan is one of my favorite desserts to make for a birthday party or a get-together because it takes no time to put together and you get to have two desserts in one. Often referred to as el pastel imposible, or the impossible cake, chocoflan is made of a creamy flan layer and a fudgy chocolate cake bottom layer. The real magic happens during the baking process: The chocolate cake goes into the pan first and then you ladle the custard mixture over it, and while it bakes, the chocolate cake trades places with the flan and floats to the top, and the flan sinks to the bottom.

INSTRUCTIONS

Preheat the oven to 350°F (180°C).

Make the flan: In a blender, combine the dulce de leche, evaporated milk, cream cheese, vanilla extract, and salt and blend until smooth, 20 to 30 seconds. Pour in the eggs and blend for another 10 seconds until smooth.

Make the chocolate cake: Sift the flour, sugar, cocoa powder, baking soda, baking powder, salt, and cinnamon directly into the bowl of a stand mixer fitted with a paddle attachment. Mix on the lowest setting until just combined, then add the softened butter and continue mixing on low speed until the mixture resembles wet sand. Stop the mixer and scrape down the sides of the bowl if needed.

In a liquid measuring cup, combine the coffee, buttermilk, egg, and vanilla extract, then slowly pour it into the flour-butter mixture with the mixer running on low. Scrape down the sides of the bowl and beat the mixture on high for a full minute.

Liberally coat a 10-cup (2.5 liter) Bundt pan with cooking spray. Add the cake batter, smoothing out the top with an offset spatula or spoon. Carefully ladle in the flan so you disturb the cake batter as little as possible. Transfer the Bundt pan to a roasting pan or baking dish large enough to fit the Bundt pan. Grease a piece of foil and place it

(continued)

FOR THE FLAN

1 (13.4 ounce/380 g) can La Lechera dulce de leche (1½ cups/355 ml)

1 (12 ounce/354 ml) can evaporated milk

4 ounces (113 g) cream cheese, at room temperature

1½ teaspoons vanilla extract

Pinch of Diamond Crystal kosher salt

5 large eggs

FOR THE CHOCOLATE CAKE

1⅓ cups (160 g) all-purpose flour

1 cup (200 g) sugar

½ cup (50 g) unsweetened cocoa powder

1 teaspoon baking soda

½ teaspoon baking powder

½ teaspoon Diamond Crystal kosher salt

½ teaspoon ground cinnamon

6 tablespoons (85 g) unsalted butter, cubed, at room temperature

½ cup (120 ml) brewed coffee

½ cup (120 ml) buttermilk

1 large egg

1 teaspoon pure
vanilla extract

**FOR SERVING
(OPTIONAL)**

Dulce de leche

Chopped nuts

Whipped cream

Ground cinnamon

greased side down onto the Bundt pan, folding it over the edges to loosely seal it. Transfer to the oven, then pour water (from the tap is fine) into the roasting pan or baking dish to come up 2 to 3 inches (5 to 7.5 cm).

Bake for 2 hours to 2 hours 15 minutes, checking for doneness after 1 hour 45 minutes, using a skewer inserted into the cake to make sure it's baked through, with little to no crumbs sticking to the skewer when you pull it out.

Carefully remove the Bundt pan from the roasting pan and let it cool to room temperature before placing it in the fridge to cool completely, at least a couple of hours.

Once you're ready to serve, carefully run a knife around any edges that are still sticking, then invert onto a serving platter, gently shaking it up and down if it's being difficult (if it was greased properly, you shouldn't have any major issues).

If desired, serve with dulce de leche and a sprinkle of chopped nuts or with whipped cream and a sprinkle of cinnamon.

Cajeta Cream Cheese Brownie Tart

Serves 10 to 12

One of my favorite things to bring back home from trips to Colima were candies. I'd bring back a little bag filled with rollos de guayaba (guava rolls), borrachitos, and bolas de tamarindo (spicy tamarind candies), but my most favorite candy of all were these little boats filled with cajeta. Cajeta is related to caramel but is a much closer cousin to dulce de leche. It's luscious, sticky, and so sweet. It is essentially goat's milk that has been reduced to a very thick and viscous syrup that you can enjoy as a topping on your favorite desserts. If you happened to be in Colima or Jalisco, you could enjoy cajeta de sayula, which would be packaged in a little wooden boat. My mom used to tease us when we were growing up, telling us cajeta came from "leche de burra," or donkey's milk, but that never deterred my sweet tooth, or me from eating any less.

In 2017, when I went to my first pop-up event as a vendor, I was armed with cajeta cream cheese brownies. I wasn't sure how they'd do since I was debuting them there. But within a few minutes, my entire pan was empty. People kept coming back for more brownies, even placing special orders; they were that good! The beautiful swirling appearance of the brownies truly makes them a work of art you can eat.

INSTRUCTIONS

Preheat the oven to 350°F (180°C).

Spray a 10-inch (2.5 cm) tart pan with a removable bottom with cooking spray, then place the tart pan on a large baking sheet.

Make the brownie base: In a medium-size saucepan over medium heat stir together the coffee, grated chocolate, and sugar, and bring to a boil. Turn off the heat and add the butter. Set aside for 5 minutes to let the butter melt and cool slightly.

After the 5 minutes, sift in the cocoa powder and stir to combine, then whisk in the eggs, vanilla extract, and salt. Stir in the flour and set aside.

(continued)

FOR THE BROWNIE BASE

¼ cup coffee (59 ml)

½ cup (70 g) grated Abuelita chocolate

¾ cup (50 g) granulated sugar

8 tablespoons (85 g) unsalted butter, cubed

½ cup (50 g) unsweetened cocoa powder

2 large eggs

1 teaspoon vanilla extract

¼ teaspoon Diamond Crystal kosher salt

⅓ cup (43 g) all-purpose flour

FOR THE CAJETA CREAM CHEESE SWIRL

8 ounces (226 g) cream cheese, very softened

½ cup (152 g) cajeta

1 large egg

½ teaspoon vanilla extract

Make the cream cheese cajeta layer: Beat the softened cream cheese in the bowl of a stand mixer fitted with a paddle attachment until it's smooth and lighter in texture, about 1 minute. Add the cajeta and stir on medium speed to combine, then add the egg and vanilla extract and stir on low speed until just combined.

Reserve ¼ cup (62.5 ml) of the brownie batter. Evenly spread out the remaining batter into the tart pan. Spread the cream cheese cajeta layer over that, then dollop on the reserved batter. Take a skewer or sharp knife and swirl the tart all around until the brownie and cream cheese are swirled and marbled together.

Bake in the preheated oven for 20 to 25 minutes, until slightly puffed and the tart is set and no longer jiggly.

Let the tart cool to room temperature, then transfer to the fridge to cool completely.

When you're ready to serve, remove the tart from the pan and serve.

Paletas de Ponche de Granada

GRANADA PUNCH ICE POPS

Makes
10 paletas
3 ounces (90 ml)

When I was little, whenever my uncles made a trip to Mexico, they would bring back a bottle of ponche de granada, which they'd drink over ice when temperatures started to soar. As I got older and finally got the chance to taste it, I realized ponche de granada was a mixture of hibiscus tea, pomegranate juice, sugar, and cane alcohol. It was sweet and sour, and it is the perfect base for paletas. I decided to omit the alcohol from these paletas because cane alcohol is not easy to find, but feel free to add up to ¼ cup (60 ml) vodka for a spiked pop.

INSTRUCTIONS

In a large saucepan, bring 2 cups (475 ml) water to a boil over high heat. Stir in the dried hibiscus, remove the saucepan from the heat, and let the hibiscus steep for 4 minutes. Strain the hibiscus tea into a measuring cup, whisk in the sugar until it has completely dissolved, then let it cool completely.

In a large bowl, whisk together the hibiscus tea, pomegranate juice, lime juice , and pinch of salt. Add 1 teaspoon of the pomegranate seeds to each of ten 3-ounce (90 ml) ice pop molds. Pour in the hibiscus-pomegranate mixture. Freeze the paletas for 1 hour, then add the ice pop sticks and freeze overnight until solid.

1 cup (30 g) dried hibiscus flowers

½ cup (104 g) sugar

1⅓ cups (315 ml) pomegranate juice

¼ cup (60 ml) fresh lime juice (2 limes)

Pinch of Diamond Crystal kosher salt

¼ cup (35 g) pomegranate seeds

Mango-Strawberry Granita

The granita is the Italian answer to shaved ice and raspados. It typically utilizes only three ingredients—fresh fruit, sugar, and water—and it takes half the effort to make. I used mango nectar and strawberries for this one to ensure I got the best flavor, and added a splash of lime juice to balance out the sweetness from the fruit.

¼ cup (50 g) sugar

1½ cups (350 g) mango nectar

2 cups (400 g) whole strawberries, hulled and sliced in half

⅓ cup (75 ml) fresh lime juice (about 3 limes)

¼ teaspoon Diamond Crystal kosher salt

Strawberry slices, for serving

Tajín seasoning, for serving

Serves 5 or 6

INSTRUCTIONS

In a small saucepan, combine ½ cup (100 ml) water and the sugar and simmer over medium heat, stirring occasionally, until the sugar has completely dissolved and the syrup begins to bubble, 2½ to 3 minutes. Remove the simple syrup from the heat then let it cool completely.

In a blender, combine the mango nectar and strawberries and blend until smooth. Strain the mixture through a fine-mesh sieve into a large bowl. Whisk in the simple syrup, lime juice, and salt. Pour the mixture into a 9 × 13-inch (23 × 33 cm) baking dish (preferably glass—if you use a metal dish, be careful not to scratch the bottom of your dish when it comes time to rake the granita), then place it in the freezer, uncovered, to freeze for 2 hours (or overnight if you're starting this the day before serving).

Rake the surface with a fork, let it freeze for another 2 hours, then rake again. Repeat this process two more times. (If you froze the granita overnight, rake the surface with a fork 1 hour before serving, then one more time right before serving.)

Serve with strawberry slices and a dash of Tajín.

Tip: For a more adult-friendly experience, serve with a 1-ounce (30 ml) shot of tequila!

Melon Granita

An aspect that I like about granitas is that they aren't heavy or loaded with sugar like raspados. They are very light, especially when you use fruits that are mostly water, like watermelon and cantaloupe. This melon granita is so light that you don't have to wait until dessert to enjoy it—it can also be served as a palate cleanser between dishes.

⅓ cup (65 g) granulated sugar, plus more to taste

2 cups (300 g) diced watermelon

1¾ cups (280 g) diced cantaloupe

⅓ cup (75 ml) fresh lime juice (about 3 limes)

¼ teaspoon Diamond Crystal kosher salt

Tajín seasoning, for serving

Watermelon balls (optional), for serving

INSTRUCTIONS

In a small saucepan, whisk together ¼ cup (60 ml) water and the sugar over medium heat and simmer, stirring occasionally, until the sugar has completely dissolved and the syrup begins to bubble, 2½ to 3 minutes. Remove the simple syrup from the heat and let it cool completely.

In a blender, combine the watermelon and cantaloupe and blend until smooth. Strain the mixture through a fine-mesh sieve into a large bowl. Whisk in the simple syrup, lime juice, and salt. If the cantaloupe or watermelon you used aren't as sweet, it might need a little more sugar. Taste and adjust here adding an extra teaspoon of sugar at a time. Pour the mixture into a 9 × 13-inch (23 × 33 cm) baking dish (preferably glass—if you use a metal dish, be careful not to scratch the bottom of your dish when it comes time to rake the granita), then place it in the freezer, uncovered, to freeze for 2 hours (or overnight if you're starting this the day before serving).

Rake the surface with a fork, let it freeze for another 2 hours, then rake again. Repeat this process 2 more times. (If you froze the granita overnight, rake the surface with a fork 1 hour before serving, then one more time right before serving.)

Serve with a dash of Tajín and garnish with watermelon balls if desired.

Tip: For a more adult-friendly experience, serve with a 1-ounce (30 ml) shot of vodka!

Horchata Granita

Granitas, just like raspados, don't always have to be fruity. This pillowy horchata granita is sweet and creamy with notes of cinnamon and vanilla. It pairs really well with rum and makes for an easy dessert that doesn't require a whole lot of attention: You simply let the rice, cinnamon, and almonds steep, then blend everything together, freeze it, and scrape it when you're ready to serve!

INSTRUCTIONS

In a small skillet over medium-low heat, lightly toast the almonds and cinnamon for 4 to 5 minutes, stirring occasionally, just until they start to turn golden brown. Then remove from heat. (We don't want to completely toast them or they'll overpower the flavor.) In a medium-bowl, mix together 3 cups (710 ml) hot (not boiling) water, the rice, almonds, and cinnamon stick. Cover the bowl with plastic wrap and let it sit in the fridge for at least 6 hours.

Pour all of the rice mixture into a blender and blend until smooth. Strain the mixture through a fine-mesh sieve into a large bowl, then whisk in the condensed milk until it has been fully incorporated. Pour this mixture into a 9 × 13-inch (23 × 33 cm) baking dish (preferably glass—if you use a metal dish, be careful not to scratch the bottom of your dish when it comes time to rake the granita), then place it in the freezer, uncovered, to freeze for 2 hours (or overnight if you're starting this the day before serving).

Rake the surface with a fork, let it freeze for another 2 hours, then rake again. Repeat this process two more times. (If you froze the granita overnight, rake the surface with a fork 1 hour before serving, then one more time right before serving.)

Garnish with a sprinkle of ground cinnamon.

Tip: For a more adult-friendly experience, serve with a 1-ounce (30 ml) shot of rum!

½ cup (50 g) sliced almonds

1 (4 inch/10 cm) stick Mexican cinnamon, broken in half

⅓ cup (60 g) long-grain white rice

1 (14 ounce/396 g) can sweetened condensed milk

Ground cinnamon, for garnish

Cucumber-Chia Paletas

Makes
10 paletas
3 ounces (90 ml)

The inspiration for this paleta came from the aguas frescas you find at the mercados and tianguis (flea markets) in Mexico. There's always so many different exciting flavors to choose from, but the most refreshing of the combinations I've enjoyed throughout my travels has been cucumber and lime with a dash of chia seeds. This paleta is sour and sweet, with some slight heat from the Tajín, and it'll leave you feeling, as my mom would say, "¡más fresca que una lechuga!"

INSTRUCTIONS

In a large bowl, whisk together ⅔ cup (158 ml) water and the chia seeds. Set aside for 15 minutes to bloom and become gelatinous.

Meanwhile, in a blender, combine the cucumbers, lime juice, sugar, and salt and blend until smooth.

Use a fine mesh sieve to strain the cucumber-lime mixture into the bowl with the chia seeds, then stir to combine. Pour the mixture into ten 3-ounce (90 ml) ice pop molds, freeze the paletas for 1 hour, then add the ice pop sticks and freeze overnight until solid.

Serve with a generous sprinkle of Tajín.

1 teaspoon chia seeds

3 cups (400 g) diced cucumbers (from about 2 large cucumbers)

1 cup (240 ml) fresh lime juice (about 8 limes)

½ cup (100 g) sugar

Pinch of Diamond Crystal kosher salt

Tajín seasoning, for serving

Bebidas

(DRINKS)

TEJUINO
Y
TEPACHE
«LAS TINAJAS»

Jardín de la Villa (2016)

Agua fresca, a refreshing fruit drink made from fruit and water with a little bit of sweetener, accompanied every meal in our household. We always had classic flavors like horchata, sandía (watermelon), pepino (cucumber), or limón, and whatever else my mom could harvest from the different fruit trees we had in our front yard. Our front yard was abundant with fresh ingredients: aromatic wild mint that I could always smell from a block away as I walked home from school, guayabas that seemed to be perpetually green and unripened, juicy ciruelas (plums), spicy chiles, and plenty of tart juicy limes all within arm's reach. The aguas frescas in this chapter were inspired by the clean, fresh flavors of ripe fruit, and we'll be making traditional aguas like agua de piña and agua de fresa, and giving other traditional flavors a fun spin, like sweetening horchata with coconut cream for horchata de coco, using sweet dark cherries for a cherry-lime chia agua, and using mint and green tea for my green tea mint and cucumber agua fresca. We'll also be making tejuino, from a sweetened atole, which has roots in pre-Columbian times.

If you enjoy a cocktail, we'll be making plenty in this chapter that you can make for celebrations, like my michelada, or my fizzy hibiscus spritzer for dinner parties or get-togethers with friends! From a delicious pineapple-passion fruit mojito that'll transport you to the beautiful beaches of the Caribbean with one sip to my dad's recipe for his Cuba (a loose riff on the citrusy Paloma) served in a clay cantarito rimmed with plenty of sea salt, this chapter is sure to have plenty of options for the perfect drink to quench your thirst on a hot summer day or to sip with your next carne asada.

Cuba

Makes
10 drinks

Mi papá is our go-to bartender when we have pachangas (lively parties), and the funny thing is, he doesn't even drink alcohol! He does, however, know how to make the most delicious Cuba, a take on Mexico's beloved Paloma. This cocktail is a blend of pineapple, grapefruit, and lime juices paired with tequila and smoky mezcal topped with grapefruit soda that mi papá likes to serve in a cantarito, Mexican clay cup, rimmed with sea salt from Colima.

INSTRUCTIONS

In a cocktail shaker filled with ice, mix together the pineapple juice, grapefruit juice, lime juice, tequila, mezcal, and sea salt. Give it a good shake, then pour it into an ice-filled highball glass or cantarito. Top the glass off with grapefruit soda, give it a stir, and garnish with a slice of lime.

2½ ounces (90 ml)
pineapple juice

1½ ounces (45 ml)
grapefruit juice

1 ounce (30 ml) fresh
lime juice

2 ounces (60 ml) tequila

1 ounce (30 ml) mezcal

Pinch of sea salt

Ice

Grapefruit soda
(I like using Squirt)

Lime slice, for serving

Hibiscus Spritzer

Makes 1 cocktail

1½ ounces (45 ml) Hibiscus Simple Syrup (recipe follows)

1 ounce (30 ml) fresh lime juice

2 ounces (60 ml) vodka, chilled

Seltzer, chilled

Lime slice or candied hibiscus flower, for garnish

The jamaica (hibiscus) spritzer is one of my favorite cocktails in this chapter—it's like a fizzy and boozy agua de jamaica! It's the perfect cocktail to make for dinner parties because it's doesn't require a lot of ingredients, you can prep the simple syrup ahead of time, and it is very light and crisp, making it easy to pair with just about any meal. You can also use the simple syrup to make a non-alcoholic hibiscus soda! Simply add 1½ ounces of the hibiscus simple syrup and ½ ounce of fresh lime juice to a tall glass filled with ice, then top it off with your favorite seltzer and give it a stir!

INSTRUCTIONS

In a chilled glass, combine the hibiscus syrup, lime juice, and vodka. Give it a stir. Top the glass off with seltzer, then garnish with a slice of lime or candied hibiscus flower.

Hibiscus Simple Syrup

2 cups water (480 ml)

1¼ cups (250 g) granulated sugar

Pinch of Diamond Crystal kosher salt

¾ cup (24 g) dried hibiscus flowers

Makes 2 cups (480 ml)

INSTRUCTIONS

In a small saucepan, whisk together 2 cups (480 ml) water, the sugar, and salt until the sugar has completely dissolved. Bring to a boil over medium heat, stirring occasionally. Once the mixture reaches a boil, mix in the dried hibiscus flowers, let it cook for 2 minutes, then remove from the heat. Let the hibiscus flowers steep for 15 minutes.

Strain the simple syrup. If not using right away, let it cool completely then transfer to a sealed jar and store in the refrigerator for up to 1 month if stored properly.

Micheladas

These micheladas are inspired by the many giant ojos rojos, or red beers, I've enjoyed in Cancún, where they mix beer together with Clamato, lime juice, hot sauce, Worcestershire sauce, and the secret ingredient, Maggi Jugo, a seasoning sauce similar in flavor to soy sauce for a refreshing concoction perfect for a hot summer day!

INSTRUCTIONS

Make the michelada mix: In a large measuring cup, mix together the Clamato, lime juice, hot sauce, Worcestershire sauce, and Maggi sauce. The michelada mix will keep for up to 1 week if stored in a sealed container in the refrigerator.

Assemble the micheladas: Spread the Tajín on a small plate. Rub a lime wedge around the rim of each of beer mug, then dip it into the Tajín.

Pour 1 cup (145 g) ice into each mug, then pour in ½ cup (120 ml) of the michelada mixture (see Tip). Top off the mug with beer, then give the michelada a stir. Garnish with a lime slice, then serve.

Tip: If you're using a glass that's smaller than a beer mug, pour in only ¼ cup (60 ml) of the michelada mixture.

Makes 10 drinks

FOR THE MICHELADA MIX

32-ounce (946 ml) bottle Clamato juice (or substitute with 4 cups of tomato juice or V8)

⅓ cup (75 ml) fresh lime juice (from 3 limes)

5 tablespoons hot sauce (I use Valentina)

3 tablespoons Worcestershire sauce

1 tablespoon Maggi Jugo seasoning sauce or substitute with reduced-sodium soy sauce

FOR ASSEMBLY

Cold beer mugs

4 tablespoons Tajín seasoning

Lime wedges

Ice

Mexican lagers, such as Corona or Modelo

Lime slices, for garnish

Horchata

Horchata is the agua fresca that was typically in our fridge when I was growing up, and back then I didn't understand how something so delicious could come from uncooked rice. Although horchata de arroz has become synonymous with Mexico, it is a drink we adopted from Spain that can be traced back to Africa! My horchata is made by steeping rice, toasted almonds, and cinnamon for a few hours before pulsing it in a blender with vanilla extract, and can be easily made dairy-free by using sugar or sweetened coconut milk to sweeten it! For two fun takes on the traditional flavors, I'm also including a recipe for horchata made with matcha (page 198), and one for coconut horchata (page 199) made with toasted coconut, coconut milk, and sweetened condensed coconut milk

Classic Horchata

INSTRUCTIONS

In a dry skillet over medium-low heat, add the almonds and broken cinnamon sticks. Lightly toast just until the almonds start to turn golden brown and fragrant, about 4 to 5 minutes, stirring occasionally to make sure the almonds don't burn. (We don't want to completely toast them or they'll overpower the flavor.) Remove from heat.

In a large bowl, mix together the rice, almonds, and cinnamon sticks, then pour in the hot water. Set aside and let rest for 4 to 6 hours. Make sure the water is hot to the touch but isn't boiling, we don't want to cook the rice.

Pour the mixture (liquid and all) into a blender, and blend for 30 seconds, then strain through a fine-mesh coffee filter (to ensure your horchata isn't chalky or grainy) into a pitcher. Stir in the cold water, condensed milk, and vanilla extract, then let chill for 2 hours in the refrigerator. Serve over ice.

(continued)

Makes
8 cups
(1.9 liters)

½ cup (55g) sliced almonds

1½ (4 inch/10 cm) sticks Mexican cinnamon, broken in half

1 cup (175g) long-grain white rice

4 cups (950 ml) hot (not boiling) water

4½ cups (1064 ml) cold water

1 14-ounce (396 g) can sweetened condensed milk

½ teaspoon vanilla extract

The Mangonada

This frozen margarita is inspired by the classic frozen treat with the very same name, sometimes called a chamango, depending on who you ask. The mangonada consists of scoops of mango sorbet topped with chunks of mango, chamoy, and Tajín, and if you wait long enough for it to soften, you can actually drink it!

FOR THE MARGARITA

4 cups (825 g) frozen mango chunks

1 cup (200 ml) mango nectar

1 cup (200 ml) silver tequila

½ cup (120 ml) fresh lime juice (about 4 limes)

⅓ cup (75 ml) triple sec

¼ cup (60 ml) orange juice

¼ teaspoon Diamond Crystal kosher salt

FOR SERVING

Chamoy sauce

Fresh diced mango (optional)

Tajín seasoning

INSTRUCTIONS

In a blender, combine the frozen mango, 1 cup (145 g) ice, mango nectar, tequila, lime juice, triple sec, orange juice, and salt and blend until smooth.

To serve, add 1 tablespoon chamoy to the bottom of a margarita glass, pour in the frozen margarita, then top with another tablespoon chamoy, a tablespoon or two of fresh diced mango, and a sprinkle of tajín.

Pineapple-Passion Fruit Mojito

Makes 1 cocktail

If you had told teenage Esteban that he'd be writing a cookbook in the future and including a recipe with a cocktail with muddled mint in it, I would have said, "¡Guácala!" Mint was one of the flavors that I wasn't fond of as a kid but that I've grown to love as my palate has changed (especially after having so many 2-for-1 mojitos in Cancún). This mojito is a blend of mint, pineapple, lime, and passion fruit that instantly transports me to one of my favorite places in the Caribbean, Isla Mujeres.

INSTRUCTIONS

In the bottom of a highball glass, gently muddle the fresh pineapple juice, rum, passion fruit puree, lime juice, sugar, and mint leaves. Add a handful of ice and top off the glass with seltzer, then stir to combine. Garnish with a few sprigs of fresh mint.

3 ounces (90 ml) fresh pineapple juice

2 ounces (60 ml) silver rum

1½ ounces (30 ml) passion fruit puree, or pulp

1 ounce (30 ml) fresh lime juice

1 teaspoon sugar

6 fresh mint leaves, plus sprigs for garnish

Seltzer

La Mula

THE MULE

3 ounces (90 ml) pineapple juice

2½ ounces (75 ml) tequila

1 ounce (30 ml) fresh lime juice

Ginger beer

Pineapple leaves or pineapple wedges, for garnish

I'm no stranger to having a cocktail with dinner in the middle of the week, especially after a long day of chasing my dogs Jepsen, Nomi, and Rigby around the house and testing a few recipes. One of the cocktails that my partner, Billy, and I have concocted while we're getting ready to sit down and watch TV is La Mula, our version of the Moscow Mule. It has pineapple juice, lime juice, tequila, and ginger beer, and it's easy enough that you can throw it together during a commercial break, so you won't miss your novela.

INSTRUCTIONS

In a cocktail shaker filled with ice, pour in the pineapple juice, tequila, and fresh lime juice. Shake vigorously for 15 to 20 seconds, then pour the mixture into a highball glass filled with 1 cup (145 g) ice. Top with your favorite ginger beer, give it a stir, then garnish with a few pineapple leaves or a pineapple wedge.

Watermelon Mint Lime Agua Fresca

Makes 8 cups (1.9 liters)

If you order agua de sandía at your local Mexican restaurant, chances are it'll consist only of watermelon, sugar, and water. It's a classic combination, but watermelon's subtle flavor actually pairs well with herbs like mint! In this recipe, the watermelon adds all the sweetness and the limes add some much-needed tartness to provide balance and bring out the watermelon's flavor, and then the mint sneaks in at the end to cool you. Hosting a party? Bring out the tequila and add 2 ounces (60 ml) of it to your glass for an easy margarita!

INSTRUCTIONS

Working in batches, place all the ingredients in a blender with ½ cup (118 ml) water and blend until combined and fairly smooth, about 30 seconds. Strain through a fine-mesh sieve into a pitcher. If your watermelons aren't sweet enough, add sugar to taste. Refrigerate to chill completely before serving. Serve over ice with a mint leaf garnish.

16 cups (2.4 kg) cubed watermelon (I used 2 whole mini watermelons, 4 to 5 pounds each)

Juice of 2 limes

30 fresh mint leaves, plus more for garnish

Granulated sugar (optional)

Cherry Lime Chia Aqua Fresca

1 pound (455 g) dark sweet cherries (about 2 cups/450 g), fresh or thawed if frozen, pitted

¾ cup (150 g) sugar

¾ cup (175 ml) fresh lime juice (about 6 limes)

1 tablespoon chia seeds

Makes 8 cups (1.9 liters)

When I was growing up, one of the few family trips we'd take every other year was to visit my aunt in Morgan Hill, in Central California, where the smell of garlic is always in the air and there are cherry trees, grapevines, and strawberry fields as far as the eye can see. Her house was on a big cherry orchard where she worked, and after spending a three-day weekend with her and mis primos, we'd come back home with more boxes of cherries than we knew what to do with. Needless to say, our fingers and lips would be stained a dark cherry red for the next few weeks until we finally finished all the cherries she'd gifted us. I still love cherries, and incorporating them into a lime chia agua fresca is one of my new favorite ways to enjoy them.

INSTRUCTIONS

In a blender, combine the cherries and 6 cups (1.2 liters) water (if using frozen cherries, you'll probably end up with some juice in the bag once they're thawed; feel free to substitute this for some of the water). Blend on high for 20 to 30 seconds until the mixture is smooth. Strain the juice through a fine-mesh sieve right into an 8-cup (2 liter) measuring cup or pitcher.

Stir in the sugar and lime juice, then stir in the chia seeds and refrigerate to chill. If you're in a hurry, make sure to wait at least 20 minutes for the chia seeds to gel. Serve cold over ice.

1½ cups (45 g) dried hibiscus flowers

8 ounces (225 g) strawberries, hulled and sliced

1 ounce (30 ml) fresh lime juice

⅔ cup (135 g) sugar, or to taste

makes
8 cups
(1.9 liters)

Strawberry– Jamaica Agua Fresca

Jamaica, or hibiscus, is one of Mexico's most popular traditional agua fresca flavors. It starts with a tea made by steeping dried hibiscus flowers in hot water, which is then sweetened with granulated sugar. I like to add pureed strawberries to my agua de jamaica—I feel like the strawberry complements the hibiscus nicely, and brings out the more fruity notes in the tea. With this recipe, I'm also including two extra recipes, one for a simple agua de fresa that is made with fresh strawberries only, and a simple recipe for classic agua de jamaica.

INSTRUCTIONS

In a medium saucepan, bring 4 cups (950 ml) water to a boil over high heat. Stir in the dried hibiscus flowers, remove the saucepan from the heat, and let the hibiscus steep for 15 minutes.

In a blender, combine the strawberries, 5 cups (1182 ml) water, and lime juice and blend until smooth. Strain the mixture through a fine-mesh sieve into a pitcher and set aside.

Strain the hibiscus tea into the pitcher with the strawberry mixture and stir to combine. Add sugar to taste. Refrigerate the agua for at least 1 hour to chill before serving. Serve over ice.

(continued)

2 pounds (907 g)
strawberries, hulled
and sliced

¼ cup (50 g) sugar,
or more to taste

2 tablespoons (28 ml)
fresh lime juice

Strawberry Agua Fresca

Makes
8 cups
(1.9 liters)

INSTRUCTIONS

In a blender, combine the strawberries, sugar, lime juice, and 1 cup (240 ml) water and blend until smooth. Strain the mixture through a fine-mesh sieve into a pitcher, then add 3 cups (710 ml) water. Give it a stir, then refrigerate for 1 hour to chill before serving. Serve over ice.

Agua de Jamaica

INSTRUCTIONS

In a medium saucepan, bring 4 cups (950 ml) water to a boil over high heat. Stir in the dried hibiscus flowers, remove from the heat, and let steep for 15 minutes.

Strain the hibiscus tea into a pitcher. Add the lime juice, sugar and 5 cups (950 ml) water and stir to combine. Taste the agua for sweetness, and add more sugar to taste if needed. Refrigerate for at least 1 hour to chill before serving. Serve over ice.

Makes
8 cups
(1.9 liters)

2 cups (60 g) dried
hibiscus flowers

1 ounce (30 ml) fresh
lime juice

¾ cup (50 g) granulated
sugar, or more to taste

Tejuino

Chances are, if you've never been to Colima (Jalisco, Nayarit, or Michoacán), you probably haven't heard of tejuino, a drink that originated in Nayarit with roots in pre-Columbian times. It is essentially an atole made with piloncillo, masa, and water, which is left in a clay pot to ferment for up to 3 days. But I prefer to use the atole right away! It is then mixed with sea salt and lime juice and poured over shaved ice to create a drink that is sure to cool you down during the hottest days of summer. I'm also including a recipe for La Tejuinera (recipe follows), a tejuino michelada inspired by a restaurant in Colima called Pikarón Cocina de Mar, where they make micheladas as tall as me!

INSTRUCTIONS

Make the atole: In a medium-sized pot or Dutch oven, bring 5 cups (1182 ml) water to a simmer over medium heat. In a blender, combine 2 cups (475 ml) water with the masa harina and salt, then blend for 20 to 30 seconds until smooth.

Once the water has begun to simmer, whisk the water while you pour in the masa slurry in a slow and steady stream. Whisking the water while the masa slurry is introduced will prevent it from clumping up. Continue whisking until all of the masa has been fully incorporated, then add the cinnamon and piloncillo. Stirring constantly, let the atole cook for 15 to 20 minutes, until the piloncillo has completely dissolved and the atole has thickened, then remove from heat and let cool completely.

Once the atole reaches room temperature, stir in the lime juice. The atole is ready to use once it has cooled. If not using right away, store in a sealed container for up to 3 days. It's normal for the mixture to coagulate after it has been sitting it in the refrigerator, so when you're ready to serve just add up to ⅓ cup (80 ml) water to the atole mixture and whisk to soften it up.

For each drink: Pour sea salt into a small plate. Rub a lime wedge around the rim of a highball glass, then dip the rim in the salt. Fill the glass with the crushed ice (it is important to use crushed ice, so it thins the drink out) and add the tejuino atole, lime juice, and a pinch of sea salt. Give it a stir, then garnish with a lime wedge and serve.

FOR THE TEJUINO

1 cup (120 g) masa harina

½ teaspoon Diamond Crystal kosher salt

1 (4-inch/10 cm) stick Mexican cinnamon, broken in half

2 (6 ounce/170 g) cones piloncillo or 1⅔ cups (365 g) packed light brown sugar

2 tablespoons (28 ml) fresh lime juice (from 1 lime)

FOR EACH DRINK

Sea salt and lime wedges, for rimming the glass, plus more for serving

1 cup (145 g) crushed ice

¾ cup (175 ml) tejuino atole (see above)

2 tablespoons fresh lime juice (from 1 lime)

Makes
7 cups
(1.6 liters)

La Tejuinera (Tejuino Chelada)

Makes 1 cocktail

INSTRUCTIONS

Pour sea salt into a small plate. Rub a lime wedge around the rim of a tall glass, then dip the rim in the salt.

Pour the atole, lime juice, and a pinch of sea salt into the glass. Add the ice, then top your drink off with beer. Give it a stir, then garnish with a lime slice.

Sea salt and lime wedges, for rimming the glass

⅓ cup (80 ml) Tejuino (see page 213)

2 tablespoons (28 ml) fresh lime juice (from 1 lime)

Pinch of sea salt

1 cup (145 g) crushed ice

Mexican lager, such as Corona or Modelo

Lime slices, for garnish

2 tablespoons (25 g) granulated sugar

2 chiles de arbol, stemmed and roughly chopped

8 cups cubed watermelon (from a 4½- to 5-pound mini watermelon)

1¾ cup (420 ml) tequila

1 cup (242 ml) fresh lime juice (from about 5 limes)

½ cup (118 ml) triple sec

3 tablespoons (29 ml) chamoy

3 tablespoons (29 ml) Tajín

Watermelon wedges

La Sandia Enchilada

THE SPICY WATERMELON

It's no secret that I'm obsessed with reality TV, especially the Real Housewives series. The girls are always out and about getting together and having drinks (and sometimes throwing them at each other), and I've noticed that the housewives of Orange County almost always specifically ask for a spicy margarita. So I've made my own recipe for a spicy margarita to enjoy with my friends while we share some hot chisme (gossip), and it features fresh watermelon, fresh lime juice, tequila, and triple sec, and is lightly sweetened with a chile de arbol syrup for a sweet kiss of heat.

INSTRUCTIONS

In a small saucepan on medium heat, whisk together the sugar with ½ cup (118 ml) water and let it come to a boil. Once it reaches a boil, add the chopped chiles de arbol, and let them cook for 1 minute then remove from the heat and let it steep for 15 minutes.

Add the watermelon, tequila, lime juice, and triple sec to a blender and blend until smooth. Use a fine-mesh sieve to strain this mixture into a 2-quart (1.9 liter) pitcher, then strain the chile de arbol simple syrup into the pitcher. Chill in the fridge for at least 2 hours before serving.

Once you are ready to serve, fill a small bowl with the chamoy, and fill a second dish with the Tajín. Dip your margarita glasses in the chamoy, then dip into the Tajín to rim the glasses. Fill each glass with ½ cup (72.5 g) ice and distribute the margarita mix evenly. Garnish with a watermelon wedge.

ACKNOWLEDGMENTS

Para mis padres, Esteban y Lilia Castillo, quienes han hecho muchos sacrificios para asegurarse de que yo siempre haya tenido las herramientas y los recursos para salir adelante.

Muchas gracias por todo lo que han hecho para mi y mis hermanos, los quiero mucho!

To my great hunk of spunk, Billy,

Hoi. I truly can't express how thankful I am to have had you by my side throughout this journey. Pacifically, I really appreciate you staying up and pulling all-nighters along with me, running out and doing grocery runs for me, taste-testing every single recipe in this book, quoting Kath & Kim at the drop of a bowler to keep me laughing, and being my rock when times got stressful. You're as thick as a thief.
I love you!

To my dogs, Mose, Nomi, Rigby, and Jepsen,

Thank you for making every day an adventure, and for always providing us with your unconditional love, especially when we need it the most. You all mean the world to me.
Mosey bear, you left us while I started writing this book and not a day goes by when I don't think of you, or sing out your name. You were the first dog I ever had, and you couldn't have been more perfect if you tried. I miss you so much, and I hope you are somewhere in heaven getting all of the carbs and cuddles you deserve.

To my agent, Dado, and my publishing team at HarperCollins:
thank you all for taking a chance on me and my work. I couldn't have brought this dream to life without any of you!

ABOUT THE AUTHOR

Esteban is a queer Chicano (Mexican-American) who lives in central California with his partner, Billy, and three dogs, Nomi, Rigby, and Jepsen. He is a communications specialist and graphic designer by day, and a home cook and reality TV connoisseur by night. He is also the author of the award-winning food blog *Chicano Eats*, where he explores his bicultural identity as a Chicano through stories and food.

As in his blog of the same name, *Chicano Eats* is a bicultural and bilingual cookbook where Castillo shares authentic and fusion Mexican recipes presented with a stunning visual sensibility. He strives to educate his readers about—and provide context behind—traditional cuisine, and also strives to redefine how people in the United States view Mexican food by presenting dishes with a very colorful and minimalistic treatment.

The book is a melting pot of delicious and nostalgic recipes, a literal mixing of cultures through food, that will act as a comfort for Latino readers who feel far from their community, as Castillo once did, and introduce the rest to flavors and ingredients they were already familiar with, prepared in a completely different way.

For more recipes, please visit www.ChicanoEats.com